THE
WOMEN'S
GUIDE TO
SURVIVING
GRADUATE
SCHOOL

Dedicated to Wilburn Hayden, Jr.,
an inspiring husband and constant friend.

—Patricia Trudeau

THE WOMEN'S GUIDE TO SURVIVING GRADUATE SCHOOL

Barbara Rittner
Patricia Trudeau

GRADUATE SURVIVAL SKILLS

SAGE Publications
International Educational and Professional Publisher
Thousand Oaks   London   New Delhi

For information:

SAGE Publications, Inc.
2455 Teller Road
Thousand Oaks, California 91320
E-mail: order@sagepub.com

SAGE Publications Ltd.
6 Bonhill Street
London EC2A 4PU
United Kingdom

SAGE Publications India Pvt. Ltd.
M-32 Market
Greater Kailash I
New Delhi 110 048 India

Printed in the United States of America

Library of Congress Cataloging-in-Publication Data

Rittner, Barbara.
    A women's guide to surviving graduate school / by Barbara Rittner
and Patricia Trudeau.
        p.   cm. — (Surviving graduate school; v. 2)
    Includes index.
    ISBN 0-7619-0389-5 (cloth: acid-free paper). — ISBN
0-7619-0390-9 (pbk.: acid-free paper)
        1. Universities and colleges—United States—Graduate work.
    2. Women—Education (Graduate)—United States. 3. Women graduate
students—United States. I. Trudeau, Patricia. II. Title. III. Series.
    LB2371.4.R58   1997
    378.1′55—dc21   97-21015

This book is printed on acid-free paper.

97 98 99 00 01 02 03 10 9 8 7 6 5 4 3 2 1

Acquiring Editor:	Jim Nageotte
Editorial Assistant:	Kathleen Derby
Production Editor:	Sherrise M. Purdum
Production Assistant:	Karen Wiley
Typesetters:	Andy Swanson/Tina Hill
Print Buyer:	Anna Chin

CONTENTS

Series Editor's Introduction

The Women's Guide to Surviving Graduate School is a welcome addition to the Sage Series "Surviving Graduate School." Written by two established scholars, Barbara Rittner and Patricia Trudeau, who themselves successfully made the transition from undergraduate to graduate student, and from graduate student to academic faculty member, this book has long been needed. The need arises from at least two factors. The first is simply that an increasing proportion of graduate students *are* women. In fact, in many disciplines traditionally dominated by men (e.g., law, medicine, clinical psychology), women are becoming the majority of new graduate students.

The need for this book also arises from the special issues of concern to many women anticipating a period of graduate study, or who are already embarked upon the journey. Examples include dealing with sexist institutions and individuals, managing childcare responsibilities, and the subtle (and not so subtle) segregation of women into particular areas of academic study or professional practice. For example, many more female than male attorneys provide low cost legal aid services; many more women practice pediatric medicine than neurosurgery; women are disproportionately represented in the ranks of child clinical psychologists compared to providers of adult psychotherapy. No doubt disciplinary differences render generalizations difficult, and the demographics of various fields are changing so rapidly as to render any summation of the present state of affairs out of date by the time it sees print. Nevertheless, females face a graduate school experience which can differ in many significant respects from that encountered by their male counterparts, often to the detriment of women.

Women graduate students are far more often than men the victims of sexual harassment perpetrated by those in positions of academic authority. Women graduate students are more likely to be robbed or assaulted than are men. Women often face greater difficulties in financing their education than men, perhaps because they come to graduate school with less initial savings; perhaps because they cannot work as many hours as men because of child care responsibilities; perhaps because departments are less willing to provide financial assistance in the form of scholarships to women. The litany could go on.

Rittner and Trudeau provide a refreshing but realistic guidebook on surviving and thriving during one's graduate school experience. From the nuts and bolts of applying and maximizing the chances for admission, to figuring out finances, planning one's course of study, dealing with faculty, and in general making a comfortable personal, social and academic life for oneself, the authors lay it all out in straightforward language and with a forthright presentation. If you are (or anticipate becoming) a female graduate student, this is *the* book to buy for yourself. If you know a woman in a similar situation, this book would make a terrific gift. I know. My wife has said how much she wishes she had read it prior to beginning her own doctoral studies. I cannot think of a more convincing recommendation than that. Enjoy this book, and best wishes in graduate school!

Bruce A. Thyer
Series Editor

INTRODUCTION

Many young women just out of college decide on what advanced degrees to pursue and what graduate programs to attend with the guidance of their professors, academic advisors and mentors, families, and friends. This book intends to address their needs as well as the issues, fears, and concerns of the returning or mature student, some of whom may have completed undergraduate work years earlier. In particular, the returning student lacks a college-based peer group to help her think through the complex decisions she faces when she begins thinking about going to graduate school. She knows she will be juggling personal, professional, and academic responsibilities but is uncertain how to best go about that without trying to do everything she always did while she takes on an academic load at the graduate level.

Deciding to go to graduate school reflects a woman's desire for personal, intellectual, and professional growth. For many women, the decision to get a graduate degree may be necessary to remain competitive in their jobs or professional arenas. Others, faced with divorce or loss of a partner, realize the economic importance of a graduate degree in supporting themselves, especially if they are still financially responsible for their children. For some women, a graduate degree is a means of upgrading professional skills or redefining expertise in an area of specialty to be more competitive. For others, graduate work promises a change in careers and an escape from a dead-end job or boring profession. For most women, the motivation to get a graduate degree involves a combination of all these reasons.

The decisions a woman has to make about getting a graduate degree (what kind, how fast, and where) become even more difficult if family and friends don't understand why a woman wants to go back to school and resist the inevitable familial, social, and economic changes that returning to school entails.

This book is organized around some basic decisions women make as they return to school. It will address

Establishing goals
Identifying school and programs compatible with goals
Selecting schools and programs
Managing the application process
Handling acceptance and rejection
Getting the whole financial picture
Selecting courses
Getting good grades
Developing support networks

This book is expected to help you learn what other women wish they had known before they embarked on a graduate degree so that you can graduate in a reasonable period of time with most of your sanity still intact. You will be hearing from them, through us, helpful suggestions they wished someone had shared with them before they started or while they were in their programs.

Last, we know you can do it. Educated women provide their families, their communities, and their professions with standards of excellence. We hope they can also have fun getting there.

1

IN THE BEGINNING

Should You Go to Graduate School?

This chapter presents guidance for women on how to decide whether to go back to school and how to choose among graduate program options. We address common concerns women have about whether to go, where to go, and when to go. We suggest ways to decide what degree or degrees best meet your dreams.

We approach these concerns from the perspectives of four women who started thinking about going to graduate school. These women are composites of many women we know, some of whom successfully survived graduate school even if the process was a little less direct than they had initially imagined.

THE EDUCATIONAL CONTINUUM

Going Forward

Many women who enter graduate school do so immediately after completing their undergraduate work and often in the same or a related field.

Gloria, 22 years old, graduated from college with a degree in psychology and a minor in child development. She finds that the job market is tight, and most of her friends have yet to find jobs in fields related to their courses of study. She realizes that she wants to counsel young children and gets advice from her undergraduate adviser. Dr. Smith suggests getting an advanced degree in developmental psychology and furthermore, recommends her alma mater.

Going Back

For some women, the decision to go to graduate school has been delayed for many personal and professional reasons.

After 20 years as an elementary school art teacher, Selina begins exploring graduate degrees in fine arts. Her passion for filmmaking was delayed by the demands of raising a family as a single mother. Over the years, she assumed more administrative responsibilities than she really wanted. As her last child graduates from college and moves into her own apartment, she finds herself thinking about going to graduate school to get a degree in filmmaking. Uncertain if she will fit in and uncertain about her ability to compete, she shares this plan with no one.

Going Higher

Many women facing changing demands in their place of work have to decide whether to get an advanced degree to remain competitive or whether to get an advanced degree to change careers.

Lonzena is 28 years old, in a long-term relationship, and has two young children. She has been working in a bank as a loan manager for the past 5 years. She realizes that only women who have masters' degrees in business administration (MBAs) are promoted. After looking over the material sent to her by the local university with an MBA program, she begins to wonder what will be involved in going back to school.

Staying Current

Many women are confronted with the reality that they may need an advanced degree to remain competitive. In recent years, more women are realizing that just to maintain their current salary and rank within their professions, they must get advanced degrees.

> Yvette, a high-level personnel administrator in a medium-sized manufacturing company, learns that her company is merging with a larger company. Uncertain of her future, she sends out her resume. Confident that her 25 years of experience will make her competitive in the open market, she is surprised to learn that without a graduate degree in human resources, she can only expect to be hired as an interviewer. Unable to relocate because she cares for an elderly mother and because of her deep roots in the community, she begins exploring local programs.

Decisions that women make about whether or not to go to graduate school are often complex and contradictory. They may well understand the professional and financial advantages of a graduate degree only to be confronted by personal and familial liabilities should they proceed. As women progress up the academic ladder, proportionately, their numbers decline. Unlike male counterparts, women are more likely to feel obligated to rationalize why they need or want a graduate degree and to be criticized for the trade-offs they have to make to complete one. In some fields or professions, women are likely to be subjected to insinuations that they are in the "wrong" field or a "male" field and encounter suggestions that they are taking the place of a male who needs the degree more.

The financial issues for women can be extremely frustrating. Many women feel the greatest need to get a graduate degree when they are the most economically vulnerable. Faced with lower earning power, recently divorced or separated women may realize that they need an advanced degree to increase earning power to survive, only to find that going to school will increase expenses at the same time it decreases the time they have available to work, consequently diminishing their financial resources.

Younger women attempting to get student loans may be asked if they are planning on getting married or pregnant or may be told they need someone to countersign the loan (preferably a male). The fact that such practices are discriminatory and illegal doesn't make them easier or less frustrating to deal with when they occur. Some women who feel uncomfortable with pressures to accept financial support from family members (with attendant explicit and implicit obligations) may defer their plans in order to accommodate partners or children or may delay their plans while they attempt to save money to cover costs and expenses. Working women may not be provided with tuition reimbursement and time off and so are forced to work part-time as they juggle school, family, and work obligations.

Because these issues often crowd together, it becomes difficult to decide whether now is a good time to go to school, what school to go to, and what degree to get. Before any decisions are made about how to finance the degree or arrange your personal life, you need to decide whether an advanced degree is something you really need or even want. In the case of Gloria, deciding to go to graduate school because the job market is tight may not be the best of reasons. Selina, on the other hand, knows that this is what she wants to do, but she may not be certain about what degree or what school will be the best one for her. Lonzena faces the dilemma of deciding whether she wants to stay in her profession and compete aggressively or whether to use the opportunity to change what she is doing. Last, Yvette is being forced to get a degree to prevent losing her job status and earning power.

In reality, every woman contemplating going back to school for a graduate degree has her own reasons for considering this decision. This chapter provides some guidelines for deciding whether you want to go to graduate school now, later, or never.

REASONS FOR AND AGAINST

Defining Personal Reasons for Going to Graduate School

Each of the women described earlier had important but different reasons for considering a graduate degree. For some women, it is a personal goal or need. Selina has used her dream of someday becoming a filmmaker as a way of making a creative future for herself. Her aspirations are not fundamentally connected to economics, although certainly making a good living as a filmmaker has an appeal. She is likely to say, "I needed to do this for me," or, "It's something I've always wanted to do." The specific degree she and similar women get may depend on what programs exist in what communities that are consistent with their personal needs.

If Selina were to have made a list of personal reasons why she wanted to go back to school at this time, it might look something like this:

Kids grown—have the time
Have great ideas for films
Love movies
Did excellent work on promotional film for the local Canadian Broadcasting
Now's the time to try it
Bored with teaching elementary school
Meet new and creative people
Need a creative outlet
Felt most creative as a student
Like freedom as a filmmaker
Think I can do it as well or better than others

Making a list of personal benefits rather than focusing strictly on the economic benefits can help you generate the kind of enthusiasm you'll need to survive the rigors of getting the degree. These reasons should be listed without concern for how they benefit others (kids or partners, parents or relatives, or even community) and because they are private, don't get too concerned with the order they are listed in or even their reasonableness. They should be your personal and private reasons to get this degree. If you find that you are having trouble coming up with personal reasons, then you will probably need very strong professional or economic incentives to keep you motivated and focused.

For Gloria, the reasons tend to be less structured:

Like working with people
Admire Dr. Smith—who is in developmental psychology
Like school
Liked psychology best and want to know more
This is the most prestigious school in the country
There are good places to ski near by
My best friend is going there and we can room together
I want to be a professional and earn $$$
I liked the tutorial with kids we did on campus
There is an active theater community nearby

Typical of many young adults, Gloria looked for an intersection between her personal and academics needs. Going to graduate school can be a good transition for someone who has just completed an undergraduate degree and is ready to move out on her own. Graduate school provides young women with an opportunity to move away from home with a combined sense of structure, familiarity, and adventure. Younger women generally experience greater flexibility about what kind of a degree to get and where to go to school.

More mature women may feel limited by their responsibilities and commitments. They often decide on programs based on the possible degrees offered locally. Getting a graduate education becomes a process of elimination—that is, how can I get a degree in an area that interests me without disrupting my entire life and the lives of my family members? Unfortunately, some women allow their personal dreams to be subsumed by their feelings of commitment and obligations to others. Therefore, making a list of how getting this degree will personally benefit you helps to reshape those commitments to include some responsibility to yourself.

A graduate degree may not be seen by others as economically necessary. You may confront overt and covert dismissal of your desires for a degree and your decision to proceed with an application. It is probably desirable to begin formulating a response to such messages and comments concurrent with the decision-making process. One of the most powerful responses is the nonresponse. We suggest a variation on the raised eyebrow, the look of total disdain that someone would make such a stupid comment, or the ever-popular raspberry (with a certain amount of sprayed saliva for maximum effect).

Many women know that for them to remain competitive in their profession or to avoid progressively narrowing their income and promotional opportunities, a graduate degree is a necessity. Some realistically feel that they have to be better educated than male counterparts to move into positions of greater power within organizations, considerations that are often valid in male-dominated professions.

> Lonzena worries that if she leaves her job to go to school, she may loose years of seniority. She seeks a program that will allow her to go to school while she remains employed. In addition, she needs to juggle child care and other responsibilities that go along with being in a relationship and raising two children.

Women are finding that the jobs they trained for originally are now being eliminated, curtailed, or downgraded. They know that additional training will permit them to find ways to use their current work experience to their advantage by having a resume with good prior work experience enhanced by a graduate degree. For them, the advanced training becomes a means of opening new doors as other doors close behind them.

Other women use shifts in personal relationships as motivations for getting graduate degrees. They may not initially identify the reasons for returning to school as outcrops of these changes but may later realize that an underlying issue was a feeling that they needed the changes that going back to school could offer. Part of the drive is to develop a stronger personal and professional identity. In addition, the need for greater financial independence can be highly motivating for women who suddenly find themselves the sole support of themselves and their families.

Is This the Right Time for Me?

There are many issues that shape the decision to go to graduate school. For many, this is a time to shift focus to meeting some of their own intellectual and professional needs. As important as those desires are, they must be considered within the context of the demands of graduate school. Getting a graduate degree is a time-consuming, if not a time-devouring, experience. It is important to consider how much time this is really going to take. Beside time spent in classrooms, you need to factor in time for labs, internships, studying, writing papers and reports, and library research. The longer you have been out of school, the more time you will need to adjust to the academic pace and to reacquaint yourself with the academic environment. Although attendance at classes may not be required, it can be very difficult to get the information you need if you aren't in class. Graduate classes often last for 3 hours or more, and you may have classes more than 1 day per week. In addition, many fields require an internship, which may require that you take the better part of a year off. It is not uncommon for these internships to have no stipends or salaries connected to them.

For those who have been out of school for a number of years, study habits have to be redeveloped. Most graduate-level classes are defined by a great deal of reading, and few faculty members are sympathetic when you are unprepared. Although we'll address some tricks to make this more manageable (see Chapter 8), most graduate students spend hours reading every week to remain current with assignments and still have to schedule time for labs, papers, and projects.

University and college library systems often require technological expertise just to learn how to do searches and to obtain material. If you aren't familiar with on-line searches and electronic data, becoming

Table 1.1 Time Planning

3 hours class
9 hours prep
4 hours for exams/papers/projects
16 hours a week per course

Based on 3-hour classes with two papers @ 15 pages each,
do I have the time do graduate work? ___Yes ___No

proficient in these areas can be very time consuming. Generally, during the first semester, you develop a pace for accomplishing everything and still having some time for yourself. Eventually, most women who make it through become skilled at dumping, shifting, and juggling the time demands being made on them. Initially, however, library work is not an area to be taken lightly because the use of libraries and electronic data sets are necessary to develop advanced knowledge in your chosen field. This is as much a part of the educational process as the classroom, and time must be set aside for studying.

Last, graduate assignments are complex and require time to do them right. Many are done in groups, and time will be needed for group members to get together to plan and complete them.

Ideally, a successful graduate student expects to spend about 2 to 3 hours of library work or reading for every hour of class time per week and about 30 hours per paper or examination preparation. To get a sense about how much time this is going to require, we've provided a formula for roughing out the weekly time (see Table 1.1). Of course, if you aren't driven to get all A's, then feel free to plan fewer hours.

If you answered yes to the question at the end of Table 1.1, then proceed to the next section. If you answered no, then think about when you'll have the time; move on to the next section, but put it under the category of future plans.

SETTING GOALS

It is important to assess what you hope a graduate degree will do for you. Making a list of the reasons to go to school *at this time* in your life (rather than 5 years from now) will help you begin to set goals.

Once you've thought globally, it is helpful to focus these statements into doable goals and then to convert the goals into concrete plans. For example, if you listed "change careers," to make it a goal statement, you need to narrow it down into components that are understandable, desirable, believable, measurable, achievable, and concrete. This will require some self-evaluation and a realistic assessment of your match with certain professions. In this case, "change careers" sounds clear, but is it really? Is anything possible? Would this include becoming a commercial jet pilot, a veterinarian, an astrophysicist? It is necessary to first list possible things that might fall into the category of change that are both desirable and achievable and in this case, require a graduate education. In addition, decisions need to be made whether change is going to build on existing skills (e.g., from accountant in banking to investment marketing specialist) or if the plan is to get out of the current field altogether (e.g., from banking to social work).

Broad categories need to be reshaped into realistic program options, and this should occur throughout the process of getting a degree. Many people start out in a program only to discover that it isn't what they expected or that they are not going to be able to do what they thought they could do with the degree. It is advisable to begin reevaluating the goals at the end of the first semester. Therefore, we suggest that the initial personal and professional goals you set should be written out and periodically reviewed.

> By the end of the first semester, Gloria hated most of her developmental psychology courses but found that her statistics courses in the department of education fully captured her imagination. She transferred into the department of education, where a subspeciality in statistics was offered. This new plan was especially attractive because she liked the community, was sharing an apartment with her best friend from college, dating a graduate student in another department, and had a part-time job. Her plan to change careers was understandable, desirable, believable, measurable, achievable, and concrete.

What Gloria did took courage. She used her first semester to reevaluate her initial goals against the program reality and within the context of her long-term goals. In this case, she found that she had set her initial goals based on her very favorable impression of Dr. Smith. By the end of the first semester, she decided that although the initial goal was achievable, it was not desirable.

Table 1.2.

Goals

Barriers to Getting This Degree

Goal setting should be an ongoing process. Few students change their whole field of study as Gloria did, but it is not uncommon for the ongoing reevaluation process to result in changing the focus or area of concentration.

In addition to identifying and clarifying goals, it is necessary to decide if there are realistic barriers to proceeding at this time. Yvette, for example, found herself thinking more about the barriers than about what she hoped to achieve with the degree. In deciding how important a barrier is, it is necessary to determine if there are resources or options available that will lessen the impact of the barrier (see Table 1.2).

FIGURING OUT WHAT YOU WANT TO STUDY

Once you've set some goals, determined that you have the time to go to graduate school, and determined that there are a few manageable barriers to completing the degree, the process of selecting a school and a program begins. This is an extension of goal setting, because deciding what school or schools to apply to is often part of the process of making the goal concrete. Each school has it's own schedule and rules, and determining which school is most likely to meet your needs is

important. Furthermore, you may be restricted to living in a particular
area and therefore must select a program available in that area.

There are some good books that can help you match global areas
of study to specific programs and will tell you if the program offers a
certificate, a bachelor's degree, or graduate levels of study (for example, *Guide to American Graduate Schools,* by Harold Doughty, published in 1994 by Penguin Press). The College Board Series has a recent
revision to their *Index of Majors and Graduate Degrees* (18th edition,
1996). This volume covers over 600 undergraduate and graduate
degrees and is organized around general topics that are then narrowed
to more specific fields within that area. You can begin to match your
goals to various schools to find which universities most closely match
personal needs and requirements.

HOW MUCH EDUCATION IS ENOUGH?

Each profession has standards of practice. In some, a doctorate is
necessary to work in entry-level positions. Other professions consider
the doctorate only the first stage of long series of assistantships and
fellowships needed to be hired at an entry level. Some require only a
certification or a bachelor degree to work in the field, and graduate
work is considered preparation for administrative work. It is helpful
to understand the role that a graduate degree has in a chosen profession before you start on one. In addition, requirements change—so be
sure to consult with someone knowledgeable about what kind of
training is needed now to do the kind of work you want to do.

After the merger, Yvette was offered early retirement at 25% of her
salary until she reaches 65 years of age. At that point, her full
retirement benefits will begin. She reevaluated her plans to go to
graduate school and decided that she would be happier as an interviewer with another company, especially because the combined income
would be sufficient to meet her economic needs. Yvette recognized
that she is not driven by professional status and was mostly worried
about the economic impact on her life style if she had to take an
interviewer position. Once she realized that the retirement package
made that less of a concern, she decided that graduate school was no
longer necessary to meet her goals.

INSTITUTIONAL CREDENTIALS

It is important to determine what credentials the school must have for a degree to be useful for you to work in your profession. Do schools have to be accredited? Does graduating from a program make you eligible for licensure or certification? In addition, if the profession requires that you do an internship or practicum, it is important to determine if the school is located in an area with sufficient placements or whether most students do placements elsewhere. The locale of the placements can increase the costs of going to school or affect the time frame to graduation. It is also important to determine whether the program offers the subspecialties that you want. Unless you are one of those people who love going to school, it is unlikely that you are going to want to do a postfellowship after graduation just to pick up needed credits.

Most undergraduates don't pay attention to what organization accredits their university. As a potential graduate student, it is important to pay attention to whether the school is a member of one of the major accrediting organizations. The brochure sent to you will often give you that information, so make a point of looking.

SUMMARY

If you think you want to go to graduate school or believe you must to be competitive, this chapter has encouraged you to do these 10 things:

1. List reasons for going to graduate school.
2. List barriers to going to school.
3. Determine resources needed to overcome barriers.
4. Reshape reasons for going to school into goals or action statements.
5. Determine if you have the time now to go to school.
6. Make a list of possible areas to study.
7. Compare the list to possible majors.
8. Determine what credentials are needed to practice or work in that profession.
9. Determine what schools offer the program you want.
10. Determine if you want to go forward now.

2

TAKING THE PLUNGE

This chapter discusses how you can increase your chances of being admitted to the program or programs you've selected. We address how to decide which schools are most likely to admit you based on your past record, and we discuss the importance of graduate record examinations, including their role in the application process. In addition, we offer hints on how to get salient information from prospective schools and how to get information about the communities these schools are located in using on-line resources.

PICKING A SCHOOL

Once you've established goals and determined that you have the time needed to go to graduate school, it is time to think about what schools are going to match your goals with your needs. Deciding where to go to graduate school involves any combination of using telephone directories, browsing comprehensive guides to graduate schools, talking to people in the know—especially faculty or professionals in the particular field—going to the library to look at university catalogs, or using a career counselor. This is the time to be as imaginative as you can be. Different schools have different things to offer, and deciding where to go should involve an understanding all of the possible options.

Many people choose what to study based on what programs are available locally. Although it is convenient to think about going to school nearby, it may not be the best choice in the long run—or even the short run. This advice is directed to mature, returning students as well as to the younger students on the high-school-to-graduate-school continuum. Before you limit yourself to one locale, think about the advantages as well as the disadvantages of relocating.

Women who are self-supporting are often constrained by costs. Cheaper schools may require relocation if you are trying to balance school fees against living expenses. Some programs, which may be fairly expensive, are located in areas where the cost of living is substantially lower than where you live now. You may find that an out-of-town school is located near family members who might let you move in until you can locate an apartment and a job. They may also become a support system to help you with locating doctors, good places to shop, grocery stores, a car mechanic, and help you with some family obligations—such as child care. On the other hand, going to school locally is far less disruptive than moving, and if you have the support of friends and family members where you live now, moving may be a poor choice.

Selecting a school should be made by assessing the advantages of staying put or relocating, without allowing yourself to feel trapped and constrained by what is locally available or dominated by what others think. It is often difficult to resist deferring to the needs and desires of others, especially for women with children still living at home, those with elderly parents or relatives needing care, those with deep roots in a community, or for those who have never been more than a hundred miles away from where they were born.

Gloria wants to relocate although her parents are resistant. They expect her to remain at home until she marries and to be an example to her younger siblings and cousins. She wants more independence, particularly because she attended college in her hometown. She discusses the reputation and prestige of the school with her parents, the advantages of getting a degree from that school, and the fact that she could easily come home for holidays and summer. She reminds them that they know and like her intended roommate and that she already has a full tuition scholarship. Eventually, her parents accept her decision.

Selina, like Gloria, feels she has a fair amount of freedom and could leave where she is living, although she feels it might be hard to sell her house, and she wonders if her children will be supportive. Her daughter-in-law is expecting her first child, Selina's first grandchild. Her son reminds Selina how much they were counting on her to help with the baby and how they worry about the baby growing up without a grandmother.

Lonzena knows that relocating her family isn't possible. Her partner was recently promoted, and the children are cared for by their doting grandparents. After discussing it with her partner and her family, she decides that finding a program in reasonable commuting distance is the only plan that makes sense for her circumstances.

ISSUES IN SELECTING SCHOOLS

There are advantages to going to graduate school somewhere different than where you got your undergraduate degree. This is especially relevant if you are staying in the same field or if you are planning on getting a doctorate. Changing schools gives you a broader perspective, allows you the opportunity to learn from a different faculty, exposes you to different types of students, enhances adaptive skills needed to cope with different environments, and increases opportunities for exposure to diverse populations. In some fields, it is assumed that going to different schools is an indication of a better educated and more rounded professional. This is especially true if your bachelor's degree is from a small school without a national reputation and you are in a highly competitive profession or want to use the degree to open doors that require the patina of prestige.

How do you go about selecting schools? As we suggested in Chapter 1, *Index of Majors and Graduate Degrees* is a good place to start and is a readily available resource. For example,

Selina, a Canadian, wonders if attending a U.S. school will open more doors than a Canadian school would because of the U.S. dominance in filmmaking. Despite the fact that many U.S. films are being made in Canada, she is afraid her degree won't be recognized by the U.S. market. She eliminates the California schools after discovering that tuition and costs of living exceed her financial means and student loan potential. Using the guide, she discovers schools in Illinois, Massachusetts, and the New York area offering graduate degrees in film that are closer to Canada in culture and distance. She eliminates Michigan, Indiana, and Minnesota because they offer only bachelor's degrees. Utah, although having programs at both master's and doctoral levels, is unappealing because travel to Canada is so difficult during winter months.

A CLOSER LOOK

After identifying schools that appear to have what you are looking for, it is important to get their catalogs so you can compare programs. Keep in mind that catalogs tend to present a glossy view of the school and the setting. It is always a glorious autumn or sparkling spring day, no one ever looks like they spent the last hour looking for a parking space, and it apparently never rains or snows on most campuses.

The first taste of reality comes when you try to get a catalog sent to you. Often the school's or department's responsiveness to an applicant can be indicative of how they treat students in general. Recognize that the end of the summer and over the Christmas to New Year period are slow times on most campuses. Some campuses operate on a 4-day week, with the campus closing down on Fridays. Therefore, when you call, try different days of the week and different times of day if you are having trouble reaching anyone at the school or department.

However, if you have to make repeated calls, if you speak only to a machine even after asking for a call back, or if you feel that you are being dismissed by the faculty and staff members when you ask fairly basic questions, it might be worth wondering what being a student would be like in that institution. Some women may respond with amusement tinged with annoyance but feel no need for personal attention as long as they get the package mailed to them. Others may find that the initial unpleasant experience shapes an expectation for an ongoing negative and hostile attitude from faculty and staff.

It is helpful to get some basic information about the program and the courses of study. Usually, the clerical support person answering the telephone is not going to be able to give you that information. If it is a program that you had rated highly but feel that you need clarification about some critical points, it may be worth trying to talk to a member of the faculty. Often, the director of admissions, one of the deans, or the director of the internships are worth contacting.

SELECTING BETWEEN PROGRAMS

It helps to know what you are choosing between, and to do that, you need some concrete information about core and elective courses, student-faculty ratios, who teaches the required and elective courses (mostly adjuncts, doctoral students, or tenured faculty members), program orientation, prerequisites, course loads, course sequencing, flexibility of programs, subspecialties, time and days that courses are generally offered, academic calendar, availability of evening classes, length of internships or fellowships, as well as the costs and miscellaneous expenses.

Be selective about how you get the information listed in Table 2.1. It is not necessary to call the dean or associate dean because many schools have this information in the brochure, and some now have the information on-line. Furthermore, you don't want to risk alienating the dean of students when you may well need him or her to authorize an exception or exemption for you at a later date.

Application fees can be hefty and references can get tired of sending out more than a few letters, so it may be best to narrow the field to at least two but no more than five schools. Once you have completed Table 2.1's checklist, you may decide to eliminate some of the schools based on factors that you have found to be inconsistent with either your goals or your needs.

COSTS

Graduate education is always far more expensive than anyone expects. There are obvious costs, such as application fees, tuition, books, and academic fees. There are supplemental costs, such as parking, computer use, shuttle fees (even if you never use it), recreation and student activity fees (even if you've never been to the student union or gym and never plan to go), health insurance and student services fees (schools are usually vague about what those fees cover), mandatory orientation, and graduation fees (even if you don't plan to attend).

Table 2.1 Work Sheet for General Information

Institution: _____

Application deadline   _____
Application fee   _____
GREs or exam requirements   _____ Yes _____ No
Transcripts requirements   _____
Number of references needed   ____1 ____2 ____3
Mandatory prerequisites   _____

Academics
    Subspecialties   _____
    Number of students/specialties   _____
    Academic year start/finish dates   __/__/__/to __/__/__
    Summer sessions start/finish date   __/__
    New student orientation date   __/__/__
    Full-time (F-T) and part-time (P-T) options   ___ F-T ___ P-T ___ Both
    Number of consecutive F-T semesters/credits   _____
    Maximum number of years to complete   _____
    Usual number of years P-T/F-T   _____
    Minimum number of credits per semester   _____
    Average number of courses per semester   _____
    Average number of weeks per semester   _____
    Average number of credit hours per course   _____
    Average introductory class size   _____
    Average advanced class size   _____

Faculty
    Number of F-T faculty   _____
    Ratio of F-T to P-T   _____ to _____
    Number of F-T women faculty   _____
    Number of women at associate or above rank   _____
    Faculty-to-student ratio   _____
    Number of F-T faculty in full-time research   _____
    Number of courses taught by adjunct faculty   _____
    Percentage of core courses taught by adjunct   _____

Graduates
    Placement services   _____ Yes _____ No
    Average graduating class size   _____
    Placement percentage   _____
    Average postgrad salary   _____

Each school has its own variations on fee structures, and you are well advised to check out all of the fees during the planning stages. Often, the department or school is oblivious to nontuition and application fees, so it is best to speak to someone in the business or financial office to get accurate information on current costs. In addition, they are often in a better position to tell you if any of the fees are targeted for increases, so be sure to ask. Some schools allow you to waive some fees if you can demonstrate that you are never going to use the services targeted under that category. It is worth discussing that before you complete the work sheet shown in Table 2.2. In addition, especially during the academic year, you can check with the graduate student association to determine if there are any fees that can be waived or any hidden fees.

Many returning students are shocked by the costs of textbooks. It is not uncommon for required texts and supplies to run $200 to $500 (U.S. dollars) per course, especially in technical fields. This includes using previously owned textbooks that are heavily highlighted and underlined (used books can be distracting, and like us, you may be mystified trying to figure out why people highlight the stuff they do). In addition, supplies are often mandatory and can be very expensive, adding substantially to the overall cost of a course. If there is a college or university bookstore nearby, it is worth checking out the cost of texts for a similar program of study, just to get a sense of what they might run for your particular area. It is a variation on a theme of new-car sticker shock.

COSTS OF LIVING

As you begin to think about each school and what it has to offer, also explore the local cost of living (see Table 2.3 for a useful work sheet). There may be trade-offs between tuition and community costs. Some schools have student housing, and that can substantially reduce the overall cost of going to a school. Some of the expenses you might want to evaluate include housing, food, entertainment, utilities, car insurance and gasoline, clothing (maintenance as well as purchasing), and so forth.

Table 2.2 Costs & Fees Work Sheet

Institution_____

Application

Application fee	$ _____
GRE examination costs	$ _____
Undergraduate transcripts costs	$ _____
Postage	$ _____
Telephone (schools, references, etc.)	$ _____
Visiting campus:	
Transportation, food, lodging, child care costs	$ _____

Academics

Tuition: Cost per credit	$ _____
Maximum F-T cost per semester/quarter	$ _____
Average text cost per course times number of courses	$ _____
Average course supplies	$ _____
Estimated copying costs	$ _____
Library fees & fines (shame on you)	$ _____
Tutoring (plan ahead)	$ _____

Fees

New-student orientation	$ _____
Registration fee	$ _____
Parking fee per semester/quarter	$ _____
Transportation fees (on-campus shuttle)	$ _____
Technology fee	$ _____
Student activities	$ _____
Student health	$ _____
Other	$ _____

GOOD ENOUGH VERSUS THE BEST

Once you have gotten information about schools offering graduate work in the field that interests you, the decision about how "good" a school to attend is a difficult one. The ranking of schools is usually based on the overall university rating, although occasionally you can

Table 2.3 Community Costs Worksheet

Local living expenses	
Total housing-apartment	$ _____
Transportation	$ _____
Food	$ _____
Clothing	$ _____
Washing/dry cleaning	$ _____
Medical/pharmacy	$ _____
Entertainment/other	$ _____
Total	$ _____

find individual rankings for programs. Basically, most schools fit into one of four categories: highly competitive, very competitive, competitive, and noncompetitive.

In some cases, the ranking of schools is done by professors currently connected with major universities who, frankly, tend to give their own alma mater the highest rating, not their present institution. Some of these institutions graduate large classes each year, which can obviously skew the results. It has been our experience that, with rare exceptions, graduates of the best schools are likely to tell you that the downside of going to those highly ranked schools is that the experience can be very stressful, and the rewards are sometimes not worth the hassles.

Very highly ranked schools are likely to want to prove that they are the most rigorous and prestigious by heaping on academic workloads. The personal as well as the financial costs of attending one of these schools may be prohibitive if you are self-supporting, especially if you must simultaneously work, care for your family, and attend school. Translation: Top-ranked schools equal lots of work, no personal life, little sleep, and increased costs.

A good education can be obtained at schools that aren't rated at the top but are still committed to producing well-educated amd skilled graduates. For women with primary caretaking responsibilities, achieving at a top-ranked school leaves little time to deal with the myriad daily demands of a busy household.

If, however, you are one of those women who easily gets everything done—bakes bread every morning before the family rises, raises an award-winning vegetable garden every year, cans vegetables for the winter, fixes your own car, repairs the roof, sews your own clothing, works a full-time job, needs very little sleep, and still reads a book a night, then go for it. Overachievers will, of course, refuse to admit that the demands of a top-ranked school cause so much as a minor ripple in their daily schedules, so avoid getting advice from them about where to go. They proudly pursue massive coronaries by age 45 and unfortunately, may not live long enough to enjoy their advanced degrees.

There is no sense in denying that going to a top-ranked school really can open doors that otherwise may only be cracked open by a degree from a second-tier school. The best schools are likely to expose you to those who are on the cutting edge of research in your given field. If you are mentored by one of the top-rated scientists or theorists in your field, you will have a distinct advantage over the rest of us in the open job market. The often heady intellectual climate of a top-ranked school and the enormous library and laboratory resources to be found in those settings should not be minimized. If you have the money and the talent to get into one of those schools and a highly charged intellectual environment is challenging and exciting to you, then it is important to explore those schools aggressively.

For many of the rest of us, going to a school that provides a good educational program at a reasonable cost and has a fairly solid placement record for its graduates is more realistic and desirable. As it is, you may want to remind your family of how they promised to be supportive (it's advisable to get it in writing), or you better hope that you win the lottery so you can hire a lot of help (at which point, you probably won't finish the degree anyway).

GRADES AND EXAMINATION SCORES

Where you get accepted is going to be based on the factors already addressed and on how good your undergraduate and postgraduate records are and how well you scored on the graduate examinations. If a school is listed as highly or very competitive and you graduated with less than an overall B+ average (or less than 3.5 quality points on a 4-point scale) as an undergraduate, then it is unlikely that you are going to be accepted unless your family has recently donated a large sum of money to the institution.

However, before you discount any school you think matches your needs and goals because your grades and scores don't look as competitive as the guidebook indicates, it is worth calling admissions to determine what their average score for the graduate examinations and undergraduate grade point averages were for the previous year's class. You can then determine if you are significantly below the lower half of the class admitted to that program before deciding against applying. Many schools will provide that information if you ask and if they can easily access it. Some schools are reluctant to disclose these figures for fear that it will appear that they are giving you the standards for admission, and each class does tend to be different. If you can convince them that you are just trying to get a general sense of how rigorous the admissions standards are for the program and you realize that the current class could differ from previous classes, you might get them to give you the figures. Often, the better the school, the more likely they are to give that information.

Even in highly competitive universities, different programs value different skills and accomplishments in their admissions profile. The kinds of community service you have done, innovations you have pioneered in an area, and the quality of your references can offset a problematic academic record to some degree.

Furthermore, don't automatically assume that if the overall university is rated as very competitive that it universally applies to all programs. Fields of study wax and wane in popularity. It is possible that when you first started thinking about going to graduate school, your area of interest was a very "hot" field. No longer the hottest major, you may well be considered for admission despite a less than stellar past academic performance.

IMPROVING YOUR RECORD

It is unrealistic to expect a school to admit you if you graduated with an overall low C grade point average (below 2.0) and your combined entrance examinations are below the 50th percentile, especially if there is nothing else outstanding in your record. If you are still determined to go to graduate school, we suggest you take graduate courses as a nonmatriculating, (*nonmatriculating* means not admitted) nondegree student or attempt another major at the undergraduate level to pull your grade point average up.

Last, the advice that your high school counselor gave you is still relevant today. Apply to one school that you would really like to be accepted to, and don't be disappointed if you are not. If you are accepted but decide on another school anyway, you can always fantasize about that great school you could or should have gone to when you are bored or frustrated in the school you are presently attending. Apply to a school you have every reason to believe you will be accepted at, and fantasize about how much more stimulating it would be if you had gone to your dream school. And apply to a school you feel should be a good stretch, and hope you get in there.

EXPLORING THE COMMUNITY

It is desirable to get some basic information about the community before you select a school. A few years ago, it was necessary to go to the actual community to look around to make an informed decision. Although traveling to a locale and staying there for a few days is still going to give you a richer sense of what being there will be like, it is also possible to do some preliminary searching using data bases. There are a couple of good resources available that you can access from most universities. Most college libraries now have access to on-line census data. You can find out how large the community is, the average household size, the median income, and the racial and ethnic distribution of the community. Many communities, especially college communities, have information available on the world-wide-web. Using the "http://www.search.com" search engine, you can enter the name of the town or city you are interested in at the prompt and get all kinds of information about the history of the community as well as information about housing, entertainment, restaurants, basic information about average daily temperatures, rainfall, and snowfall, and the role of the college or university in the community. You also can tap into the university's web page (most now have one) to further refine your information on the kinds of resources the university has available to students. This includes student housing, financial aid, religious organizations, on-campus dining, women's organizations, theater and entertainment sponsored by the school, team sports, and program-specific information. Getting these specifics is especially important if you don't know anyone who has ever lived or gone to school there. If you don't know the first thing about cyberspace, now is the time to ask one of your friends' kids to show you around the world-wide-web pages.

If you are planning to visit the area, contact the schools because they usually know which hotels or motels have favorable rates with the university or college, places that are close to the university, near main roads, or easily accessible to the airport so you can minimize some of your expenses. We also recommend that if you do visit, try to arrange to meet with faculty, especially those in your expected major field of study.

SUMMARY

Where you get in to graduate school has a great deal to do with how you go about evaluating your strengths, weaknesses, goals, and desires against the many possible options. As tempting as it may be to select a program based on what is available locally, it is our recommendation that at this point in the process, you explore as many options as you can. Be as imaginative and creative as possible about considering all of the programs in the area or areas that interest you.

Before you make any final choices, it is important to get information about the schools beyond what you are told in the glossy literature put out by the university and the program. In particular, you'll want information about what it will be like to be a woman in the program. Will you be taught by women, do women have a strong presence on the faculty, will you have access to the faculty of national reputation that drew you to the program in the first place, does the program have subspecialties that interest you, and is financial support available— these are just a few of the questions you will want answered as you try to differentiate one program from another.

This is definitely the time to assess the costs involved against the advantages of each school. Keep in mind that there are both economic and professional advantages and disadvantages to going to a top-ranked school that must be considered on an individual basis.

Last, once you have narrowed down your selection, keep in mind that there is more to your admission package than your grade point average and your entrance examination scores. You may need to deal with a very marginal undergraduate record before you begin applying to graduate schools. Although your whole package will be considered, if you graduated from college with a low C or D average, few graduate schools will take your application seriously.

In graduate school, you will be developing expertise in a particular area. It is important that you choose programs that closely match your career goals and plans, that are academically rigorous enough to make you competitive when you graduate, and are located in communities that have the social and cultural resources you need.

3

THE APPLICATION PROCESS

We begin by reminding you of the obvious. A well-prepared, clear, and complete application package can only be an asset in the application process. Most people know that good grades and high graduate entrance examination scores are important. As good as your scores might be, you can compromise your position by filling out the form incorrectly or poorly, by leaving out important information, or by having the wrong people write letters of reference.

Read the total application package over carefully because the materials in there provide a good source of additional information about what kinds of things that program or school considers to be important. Begin by reading the overview of the program carefully. Make sure this program has the focus you want and that it will lead to what you want to do. The descriptive materials will give you a great deal of useful information about the orientation of the program within the profession. It is worth making note of buzzwords or phrases they use to describe the program. If an essay is required, keep what you've read in mind as you formulate themes for the essay and incorporate the buzzwords and phrases creatively but appropriately.

COMPLETING THE FORM

Next, pull out the application form itself. Check each line for the exact information that line requires before you begin to fill it out. You may need to assemble various documents before you start. An application can be downgraded if there are too many cross-outs or errors on the form. Most admissions committees will see it as indicative of poor attention to detail, an undesirable trait in graduate students. Avoid using faded ribbons or a typewriter with worn-out and ink-clotted letters. If you are not skilled as a typist, you are likely to type above or below the lines and have multiple type-overs. The impression a poorly typed application conveys is that you will produce sloppy work. Not everyone is good at filling out forms, even if they try to be very careful. If it turns out that you always have problems filling out forms, you have two fairly painless options: (a) Make a few extra copies of the form and practice before you complete the final version, or (b) get someone who is really good and has a great typewriter or enviable handwriting to fill it out for you.

You can choose to leave out any information concerning gender, date of birth, marital status, financial status, and national origins that you want to omit. However, you do have to complete information about when and where you graduated from high school and college, about related work or volunteer experience, and about any past criminal arrests if the form requests the information and you sign a statement that the enclosed information is accurate to the best of your knowledge. In many programs, falsifying application material can be grounds for immediate dismissal if the misrepresentation is discovered, regardless of how stellar your performance has been while in the program.

In other areas, your reporting responsibilities are less clear. There is legitimate debate about when and under what conditions you should provide information about disabilities, including substance-use histories, or medical (including psychiatric) histories. Depending on the field you are pursuing, that information may or may not be important or relevant.

Many programs request that applicants provide explanations about certain past or current conditions. Programs encourage you to explain the circumstances fully or provide comprehensive information about the current status of the problem. In some cases, they are attempting to determine if you will need reasonable accommodations because of the condition. In other cases, they may be attempting to determine if you might be a liability to the program. Be judicious about what information you do provide. It is neither necessary nor appropriate for you to give extensive details about your injuries, the relationship you have with your therapist, or the current status of your law suit unless that specific information was clearly requested. It is important to give a clear picture of whether or not the condition is likely to cause any academic limitations, restricted settings for internships, or postgraduation employment problems or whether you are likely to need reasonable accommodations or leaves of absence.

Arrest records are even more complex issues. At one point, being arrested for antiwar activities was likely to exclude you from getting into any school with U.S. National Defense Loan programs. A few years later, antiwar arrests became a badge of honor, and schools ceased concerning themselves about students with related arrest records as long as they were at the misdemeanor or third degree felony level. However, most schools are cautious about admitting those arrested for felony offenses and convictions without clear evidence that the person has been rehabilitated and poses no risk to the institution. This is particularly important if the program places you in an internship or graduates you to practice in an area where your past record prohibits you from practicing. If the school expects that your arrest history will have a bearing on your ability to be licensed or certified or that the school might be held liable for any actions taken against you while you are in the program, they may not admit you. They will probably discharge you from the program for cause if they find out you have falsified your application, regardless of your performance in the program.

Some words of warning: When addressing the area of concern, do not be vague or evasive about the circumstance or the condition in your explanation. Most faculty members reviewing applications usually recognize when explanations are needed and when they aren't being provided. Equally important is for you to recognize that graduate school is not a good place to work through personal, emotional, marital, or other problems. The demands of graduate school often increase rather than decrease stress levels and exacerbate rather that resolve those problems.

DECLARING A DISABILITY: PROS AND CONS

If you want or need to receive reasonable accommodations because of a disability, you should contact the school's office of disability or special needs to find out how that is done and what kinds of accommodations are possible. If such a number is not listed, usually the school's general information person can tell you how it is done at that institution.

Larger universities, in particular, can make a remarkable number of accommodations, including fully accessible environments and residences that are designed for visually and hearing impaired students as well as those with ambulatory restrictions. Readers are available to help visually impaired and learning disabled students. With sufficient planning, they can make tapes of textbooks and articles for courses, though most graduate students find that graphs and tables are hard to translate into audio tapes. In addition, readers are available for examinations and for material that is put on chalkboards by instructors. Some programs provide signers (translators proficient in sign language) for those with hearing problems. Many larger campuses have special computer sites with voice synthesizers and specially adapted printers, keyboards, and screens for those needing Braille conversion printouts, very large print, or less responsive keyboards. Because not all classrooms on campus are likely to be accessible, especially in older schools, letting the school know in advance what you need can make it possible for both of you to plan ahead.

However, as an obvious and we hope unnecessary reminder, the decision to be identified as a person with a disability is entirely yours. If you are disabled and need accommodations, then declare it using the process identified by the university to do so. If, however, you are blind and hearing impaired or suffer from serious learning and physical disabilities and you don't want to be identified as disabled, then you are not and cannot be so labeled. Of course, you also cannot request any special accommodations.

If you need accommodations, you should get some information in advance about how accessible the environment is, whether the services you need are provided, and how receptive your department is to those with disabilities. Frankly, some disciplines are much more accommodating than others, and some departments in an otherwise unaccommodating institution can be the exceptions. If you are uncertain about whether a campus is generally responsive, it is advisable to get in touch with local branches of such organizations as United Cerebral Palsy or those for epilepsy and multiple sclerosis. If they aren't listed, try the Department of Vocational Rehabilitation. They usually know how good the school is at meeting the needs of those who are disabled. They often can give you very salient information about the general responsiveness of the university or college and even might be able to provide more specific information about various schools or departments.

A final word of caution: Be realistic about your potential limitations. If the discipline you are interested in has a heavy emphasis on abstract thinking and advanced mathematics and your disability involves significant learning problems in that area, it is not likely that the program will be able to provide you with sufficient accommodations to ensure that you will graduate with the knowledge and skills necessary to be effective in the field. The issue is whether there are reasonable accommodations that can be made. As one person, with postpolio bilateral paralysis, so eloquently put it, "No amount of accommodations can make it possible for me to be a firefighter."

GRADUATE EXAMINATION SCORES

Let us get this out of the way up front. Some people are terrible examination takers. They freeze up and experience brain drain the minute someone puts a number 2 pencil in their hands and tells them to open to page 1. These are the very people who are likely to be accused of cheating because they misspell their name on the form.

If practice makes perfect, then taking the entrance examinations a few times could raise your points. Usually, all of the scores are reported, but if the scores keep going up, schools may recognize it as examination jitters. Hopefully, as you become more familiar with the test and the way it tends to structure the questions and answers, you will do better. Some graduate schools take the best subscale scores to compose a total overall score for the student, which can be to their benefit.

These tests have become a screening tool, which admittedly most commonly screens in good test takers and screens out poor test takers. In some academic fields, that may be a legitimate use for them. How schools use the scores varies dramatically from school to school. Some schools decide who to admit primarily on a combination of your scores on these tests and undergraduate grades; other schools weigh the scores based on when the applicant graduated from undergraduate studies because they assume that recent graduates are more adept at multiple choice questions than those who graduated 20 years ago.

In reality, admissions offices get more stupid questions asked about graduate examinations than in any other area. For example, one applicant wanted to know if her sister's score could be used, "because everyone says we are exactly alike." Another applicant wanted to know if we would accept scores from only two of the three test areas because they ran out of time in one section "so the analytical scores shouldn't count." Another applicant wanted to know if we would accept her college entrance board scores from 1963 in lieu of a current Graduate Record Examination "because I know even more now."

The bottom line is that if the school uses these examinations as part of the application, then they are going to count. You need to make sure that you do the best you can on them. If you don't want to invest in one of the examination preparation courses, then at least get the test guide books so that you can practice taking tests before the actual examination date.

These days, you can take the graduate school tests via computer. Taking them this way is useful if you are computer friendly but could be a potential disaster if you aren't. The advantage of taking the examinations via computer is that you get the results immediately. If your scores are good, then you don't have that to worry about anymore. If you didn't do well, you'll know if you have to sign up for a preparation course or study in a particular area to improve your scores.

PREREQUISITES

Most graduate programs have inflexible rules about prerequisites. These rules are usually dictated by the accrediting or professional organizations, and few are negotiable. It's important to read the descriptive material and the application form carefully to make sure that you have the prerequisite degree or that you have taken all required undergraduate or graduate courses. It is sometimes possible to begin a required course at the same time you start a program, but that is something you have to clear before you make any such assumption. It is advisable to get such agreements in writing because that person may later deny making any such agreement. In addition to the specifics, make sure you get time frames clarified. Make clear if it must be done before certain courses are taken or whether it can be taken at any time as long as it is taken before the degree is conferred.

Occasionally, an applicant has taken course work in the same field at a different institution or in a related field at a graduate level and wants to apply the credits toward this degree. Generally, schools are willing to consider doing that, though usually it is unallowable if the credits were applied toward a completed graduate degree in another field. Expect that the number of credit hours that can be transferred will be very limited. In most institutions, the grade and quality points are not included in transferred credits (unless taken in the same institution), although the grade received in the course usually must be at a B or higher level. Last, it is a mistake to think that courses are interchangeable. Every discipline and most schools have their own orientation to subject matters and they may, in fact, take exception to the orientation of a closely related discipline especially if they are essentially competitive fields.

APPLICATION ESSAYS

Essays are a very important part of the application package. They help the admissions committee assess many things about you as a person and as a potential scholar. Do not throw something together the day before the application deadline unless you are a very gifted thinker and writer.

We suggested earlier that you review all of the material sent in the application package before outlining the essay. The material will help you think about the language used in the profession currently, the program's buzzwords, and the issues that the faculty at this institution are likely to feel are important.

Before you start writing, try to determine what things the admission committee members are going to be screening for when they review your application. If you had an opportunity to visit the school and meet with faculty, review the information you were provided and incorporate relevant materials from the interview into the essay. Do not, however, exaggerate or misrepresent your experience, skills, or accomplishments and avoid obvious pandering. Faculty may have fairly big egos, but they are rarely fools. The purpose of the essay is to give the committee information that makes you an appealing candidate.

If you have been asked to explain past history, do so in a straight-forward manner to clarify what you have been doing since the condition developed or incident under question occurred. It is important for the committee to understand, as succinctly as possible, what impact the occurrence has had on your life, what you learned from it, and how it will affect your academic and professional performance. Be realistic, be clear, be honest, be appropriate, and be brief.

Your essay tells the admission committee if you understand what kind of a program you are applying to and whether you have realistic goals that are consistent with the profession and the school. Obviously, your writing skills are going to be evaluated in the essay. Demonstrate that you can follow directions by using headings that orient the reader to where you are in the outline. Make sure that you follow all of the directions and cover all of the topics requested. Keep your answers focused and related to the profession or discipline, and make sure you stay on topic. Simple sentences read better than complex and run-on sentences. Some great writers, such as Faulkner, have gotten away with page-long sentences, but they are the exception. Do not use a word listed in the thesaurus unless you are certain it is a good choice. Screen for repetition of the same word in the same paragraph. Either tighten the sentences to eliminate words or find appropriate alternatives. The two most overused words in these essays are "really" and "very." Under no circumstances should you exceed the page limitation. Faculty members do not want to read your life story. They also do not want "factoids" that barely address the requested information.

Use proper spelling and grammar. Most computer programs have a spell-check feature. As a result, faculty members are less tolerant of spelling errors than was true during the period of handwritten or typewritten essays. Make sure that sentences and paragraphs are organized and have a logical sequential flow to them. Demonstrate that you can write paragraphs that build a theme. If you use a metaphor, stay with it throughout the paper. Last, use white paper; it looks more professional than colored or watermarked paper.

Reread the essay a week after the final and edited version has been completed. This will allow you to pick up grammatical errors, inconsistencies, redundancies, and unclear sentences.

This is not one-time advice. In most graduate programs, thoroughly researched and conceptualized, well-organized, and tightly written papers are the norm. Good papers take time to write and polish. Mediocre papers that you produced for Bs in college may be failed outright or returned as unacceptable in graduate school.

Keep in mind that many schools use the essay to weed out those who tend to blend their personal and professional lives. Before you mail off the final version, reread it to decide if you have written anything you would not want announced on a public loudspeaker at a major league ball game. You need to make an effort to keep your personal and professional lives separate. Therefore, unless you are responding to requested personal information, keep it professional. Last, make sure that you submit the exact number of copies requested.

Once again, it is important that you take your time with the essay. It is going to be carefully read and, therefore, it should be carefully written. It is inadvisable, and it is unethical, to have someone ghost write the essay for you. If an essay is required for admission, you can expect to be taking a lot of essay examinations and writing a great many papers if you are accepted. Poor writing skills can severely compromise your performance and can result in your dropping out or failing out of a program. It is probably worth going to a writing skills course (many universities and colleges offer them) before you embark on a graduate program if your writing skills are not good. Getting in is great, but you also have to survive the demands for written work to succeed in the program.

LETTERS OF REFERENCE

Getting good letters of reference are crucial to a successful application. Who you select is almost as important as what they say. The purpose of the letters is to get professional opinions about your abilities to succeed in an academic environment and your ability to do the work you want to be trained to do.

Begin by thinking about teachers you had as an undergraduate who are likely to remember you. If you have worked or volunteered in a related field or capacity, your supervisors or coworkers are good choices. Do not ask your next door neighbors, religious leaders, or your personal mental health or medical provider to write letters of reference unless you have also worked directly with them.

> Gloria helped start an inner-city tutoring program through a campus-affiliated church. When she asked for a reference from the pastor connected to the volunteer project, it was appropriate. She also discussed with him that she needed a letter that would describe her skills in working with children and her knowledge about the effects of poverty on children.

It is important to be clear with the person why you have asked them for a reference. This calls for either a telephone call or a cover letter. Tell the person if you want the letter to highlight your academic achievements, ability to take on difficult tasks, relationship with authority, diligence and attention to details, ability to work in a team, organizational skills, or your clear passion for the field of study or all of these areas.

When using faculty members, try to use full or associate professors before asking assistant professors or instructors. This assumes at your undergraduate program you had classes with senior faculty. Do not use your high school faculty unless you need to prove a lifelong interest in the field. The school may interpret it as indicative of a poor relationship with college faculty members. If you have taken graduate courses either for a degree in another area or as a nonmatriculating student, then use faculty from those courses.

In some cases, you need to remind the person what course you took from them, where you generally sat, and anything you can think of that might trigger their memory of you. Some faculty members never learn the names of students, so your name alone may not be meaningful. If you plan far enough in advance, it is probably worthwhile holding on to a few very good papers or examinations from each class and offering to send a pertinent copy to the chosen professor. If nothing else, the person is likely to be flattered that you still have work from the class you took with him or her.

Nonfaculty members are a little more difficult to coach about what ought to be in the letter. If you have a work history, supervisors and administrators are usually good choices as well. They can add some depth to the material on you in the admissions package. If you do ask a past or current supervisor to write a letter, make suggestions about what kinds of information will be useful to academicians. Schools are more likely to be concerned with how you manage time, your creativity and innovations, your relationship with clients, supervisors, and coworkers, your ability to handle stress, your energy and enthusiasm, and your attention to detail. Suggest global statements rather than those focusing on your knowledge of a particular product or function or your knowledge of policies and procedures in the industry.

Unless the school specifically asks for personal (nonprofessional) references, it is advisable to avoid them. If, however, that is your only option, then it is important to help the person writing the letter understand exactly what kind of program you are applying to and what kinds of information would be relevant for them to put into a letter. Avoid "warm and fuzzy" letters about what a nice person you are. Instead, ask them to focus on your drive and ambition as well as your integrity.

Remember, it is important to follow up with all of the people you have asked for letters about 2 to 3 weeks before the application deadline to determine if the letters have been sent. Late letters can invalidate your application. Therefore, make sure that you have an alternative person in mind who can write one for you in a hurry. It is better to have one more letter of reference than is required. Most schools will file all of them, though some might ask you to select among the ones received.

Be sure to call or write a note to express your appreciation to each person who wrote a letter on your behalf. Besides being the right thing to do, you never know when you are going to need them to write another letter for you.

THE INTERVIEW

An interview is required by many schools, although for out-of-town students, the interview can be usually conducted by telephone. You should prepare for the following most frequently asked questions:

Tell me a little about yourself.

Why do you hope to accomplish with this degree?

How did you selected this profession, degree, university?

What will be your area of subspecialty? Why?

What are your strengths and weaknesses?

What courses did you excel in as an undergraduate and why?

Tell us about your related employment history.

There are some advantages to rehearsing answers to these questions. You will sound very articulate. In addition, you will appear more confident than many of the people they will be interviewing. If you are applying for a technical program, make sure that you either bring examples of your work or can easily and flawlessly articulate some technical material. In the fine arts, ask professionals to help you put a portfolio together that will demonstrate the range of your skills and potentials.

Remember that when you arrive for the interview, the faculty members will expect you to dress appropriately. It may seem inequitable that they are in jeans and sandals while you are mentally tugging at stockings, but it is worth slightly overdressing rather than seriously underdressing. The more formal the community, the more formal your dress should be.

Do not get into personal matters. The fact that the person interviewing you asks questions does not mean that you have to answer them.

> Selina was asked if her family was concerned about her moving to the States. The fact that she discussed the situation with her children wasn't any more the interviewers' business than the reasons she chose not to stay in Canada. She responded by saying, "I presume that you must be concerned about whether I have the appropriate immigration forms. I have made all the proper arrangements for a student visa, which should be on file in my folder."

It is tempting to get invited into personal discussion, but it is as much a mistake in graduate school as it would be in a job interview. Keep your boundaries well-defined and clear from the beginning, and you will have less problems later on trying to establish them. Do, however, answer questions about your educational and work experiences, what courses and tasks you like the best, how you handle stress, and what your long-range plans are. Do not talk about your marriage, your childhood, your religious beliefs, or your physical or mental health (unless you are asking for special accommodations).

REVIEWING THE COMPLETED APPLICATION

At this point, you are ready to mail out the application. Make a check list based on all of the application requirements. Make sure that the form, the essay, and the check are enclosed in the envelop. Call your references to check with them about when they sent off the letter of reference. Make sure that when you send off for the undergraduate transcript to be sent to each school, you include a postcard for them to send back to you indicating the date the transcript was mailed. Make sure you have everything ready at least 2 weeks before the deadline. Make sure you address the envelope correctly. Read the directions carefully, and use proper codes to ensure that it gets delivered to the right department. Rather than folding up the materials and overstuffing an envelope, it is advisable to spend the few extra cents to send it in an appropriately sized manila envelope.

Do not try to guess the weight and the postage, because guessing wrong will result in the material being returned to you for additional postage. It is not advisable to request a return receipt if the envelope is addressed to a person because the mail carrier may insist on the addressee signing for the package. If he or she is out of town, receipt of the package will be slowed down. Place a self-addressed and stamped postcard inside the envelope with a Post-it requesting that it be sent to you when the package is received. Some schools automatically notify you when they receive the package, but some women need to be certain that it has been received.

Do not keep calling to find out if the package has arrived; the administrative support person handling the applications is usually buried under mounds of paper work during the 2 weeks before the application deadline, and telephone calls are considered unwelcomed and unnecessary intrusions.

Keep in mind that there are many advantages to getting your application reviewed early in the general screening process. Most schools farm them out to faculty members for review as they come in, regardless of the deadline. Early applicants aren't as likely to be compared with other, potentially better, applicants. Therefore, the weaker your application, the more important it is for you to get your application in early so you don't pale in comparison to stronger applicants. The best time is about 3 weeks before the deadline. That way, you are likely to be reviewed in the initial run of applicants but not so early that faculty members have time to scrutinize the details of the package more thoroughly than you would want.

SUMMARY

Now that you've tentatively made a commitment to apply for a graduate degree, let us summarize the steps in a successful application:

1. Line up the people you need for references, remembering to be appropriate in the selection.
2. Obtain catalogs and program application packages.
3. For each application, review the package for specific information you will need.

4. Request that transcripts and graduate examination scores be sent to each school.

5. Contact faculty members who you feel would remember you, and ask them to write letters of reference. Remind them who you are, tell them how much you enjoyed their courses, and if possible, offer to send copies of work you did for their courses.

6. If you haven't access to faculty members, then coach nonfaculty references on the kinds of things the schools probably want to know about you.

7. Complete the application carefully. Pay special attention to the outline given for the essay. Your writing will be evaluated on both your ability to follow directions and your ability to write at a graduate level. The content in the essay should reflect your long-term and future commitment to the profession or field and avoid highly personal material unless it is specifically requested in the application material.

4

TO BE IN OR
NOT TO BE IN

In this chapter, we discuss what to do if you are accepted—and uncertain if that's the school you want to attend, what to do if you are rejected—and that is the school you *really* want, and what to do if you are unable to attend.

THE WAITING GAME

Once the applications have been mailed, the waiting begins. For those who have been out of school for awhile, you will be surprised how anxious you become. For some, there will be a sudden eruption of acne, even if you haven't had an outbreak in years. You may find yourself alternating between excitement and a sense of dread. No matter how often we, or anyone else, reassures you that it is a normal and shared experience, it doesn't seem to relieve the symptoms.

On the other hand, a few women seem to become completely calm once the process is no longer in their control. They tuck it into the back of their minds and only think about it while standing in lines, going for the mail, or waiting in traffic.

No matter how you experience waiting, it is going to seem like a long time. The reality is that most schools need about 2 to 3 months from the closing date to decide who to admit. Generally, they begin notifying applicants between April and June whether they have been accepted for the coming academic year. Therefore, the period between applying and being notified is a good time to go on vacation or buy some trashy novels so you can enjoy your last remaining opportunity for leisure time activities. Once you start graduate school, it may be a long time before you'll be reading anything for fun, and you will find that you are almost too exhausted and poor to enjoy time off. In reality, this is a good time to do things you enjoy and that are nonstressful. You'll soon have enough stress in your life surviving graduate school.

It is surprising how many women begin the wait by devaluing themselves and the things that they want most. They begin to assume either that they aren't good enough to get in where they applied or that they won't be good enough to succeed if they are accepted. It is important to remember that if you want to go to graduate school, it is likely to be because you are talented enough, bright enough, and motivated enough to succeed. These are important characteristics in a successful student, and most schools are aware of what it takes to get a candidate through the program. If they accept you, it is because they believe you will succeed.

WHILE YOU WAIT

Before you get engrossed in the trashy novels you've bought, establish a first choice and a fallback list of the programs. This will serve as a guideline to help you sort out the acceptance (and possible rejection) letters.

Why is this list important? Realize that one school may accept you but not provide you with the financial support you need to meet tuition and costs. Another school may put you on a waiting list but fail to give you a ranking on the list. A third may accept you into a program unconditionally, give you a tuition break, but provide no additional scholarship monies in an extremely expensive community. You're going to need some way to sort all of this information so you can make a decision you can live with in the short-term and long-term.

Make a list of all schools, ranked by how the academic program, the community, and professional achievements of the graduates match the list of goals you made for yourself in Chapter 1, without factoring in any financial breaks, economic support, or other conditions. Make a second list based on the same rankings with tuition breaks, scholarships, and loans included. Make a final list in which you rank where you would place the school if you got on their waiting lists. If possible, try to see if there are matches in the first three (if you have applied to five schools) or the top two (if you applied to three schools) on each list. This way, you can develop priority schools so you can decide what to do with acceptances rather than just accepting the first school that accepts you.

ACCEPTANCES AND UNCERTAINTIES

The first acceptance you get is usually followed by a sense of relief and excitement. That school may look very good the moment you read, "We are pleased to inform you that . . . " This may be the case even if the school was at the bottom of your list. If you are one of those who approached this with self doubts, you will feel relieved that you can go to graduate school (even if you foolishly devalue the school for accepting you). It may be tempting to accept outright and be done with it when that first letter comes in, but this is a serious decision and deserves more careful consideration. We suggest waiting for at least one more response to get a sense of your choices before you send back a check and a letter of intent to attend.

Remember that the first school to respond either may be more efficient or more desperate for students. "Efficient" is great; "desperate" may imply serious limitations. You want to make sure that this educational experience is informative and rewarding at multiple levels. As each school's acceptance comes in, review the priority list you've made, and ask yourself how effective that school will be in helping you achieve your personal goals with their curriculum. That is why you made that list suggested in Chapter 1. Make sure the list is posted someplace prominent, and as each letter comes in, check the school's ranking on the list. Goals are critical to a successful graduate degree process, and it is important to remain goal directed so that the degree does not become an end in itself and the goals become secondary.

Hopefully, you will get into all of the schools you applied to, but you won't necessarily know for some time. This becomes especially frustrating because most schools have acceptance deadlines. Not all schools allow you to accept and then withdraw without penalty, and those penalties are usually in the form of nonrefundable deposits that are sent in with your letter of intent to attend.

If you are too hasty in turning down those at the bottom of the list, you could find that you regret it. This is especially true if the school you rejected turns out to be the least expensive or offered you the best scholarships. In rejecting that school too hastily, you may also be turning down scholarship money you will need. There are always more students needing money than there is money available, so schools are anxious for information from you about you commitment to attend, especially if you are going to need scholarships and loans.

If you are certain that you are going to need financial help, you may have to accept a school offering you the support you need, even if you aren't certain that's where you will attend. That also means that you are going to have to send in the deposit as well. Consider it part of the cost of graduate school. Obviously, if your top school responds first or early with a great scholarship, then all of this is moot.

Some frustrating and subtle uncertainties may arise. In the span between when you applied to a program and the letter of acceptance, you may have decided on a different focus of study. The desirability level of a school may shift after you apply. It is important that you update your ranking of schools as your circumstances change.

> Selina's granddaughter was born as the letters of acceptance began arriving. The event had a greater emotional impact on Selina than she anticipated, and she altered the ranking of the schools to accommodate her desire to be a part of her granddaughter's early years. The school she had applied to in Boston, which initially was her fallback school, shifted to the top of the list. She appreciated the easier travel to Toronto from Boston than from New York City, where her previously first ranked school had been. She also realized that the school in Boston had been doing some very innovative digital arts programming, an area she had been exploring in recent months.

It is imperative that you reevaluate your educational goals throughout this process. They will often include a combination of personal and professional issues. At different times, each of those issues may reach ascendancy.

It is not uncommon for people to experience cold feet as they move into having to commit to graduate school. For some women, this is a reflection of the devaluation of education for them. The more that the field you have selected has been identified as a so-called male field, the more likely it is that you will experience concerns about your ability to compete. That is one of the reasons we recommend writing down your goals and revisiting them often. If you were goal directed enough to apply and the school believes you are goal directed enough to succeed, then it is important that you reject these uncertainties as soon as they arise. The only use they have is to hone your competitive edge.

WHY RESPONDING EARLY COUNTS

This is a time to be selfish but within social limits. It is important that the moment you know for certain that you are *not* going to attend, you notify those schools immediately. Remember that most professions are like small towns: Bad behavior has a way of getting around. Not showing up after you have accepted is bad form if you have not notified them in a timely manner of your withdrawal. You are effectively denying someone else admission to the program, and you are reducing the size of the admitted class, which for the school is a serious economic issue. The consequence may not be immediately apparent unless you decide to go on for a doctorate or to teach as an adjunct and suddenly discover you are persona non grata. By having a hierarchy of schools in mind, as you get accepted by the schools at the top of your list, you can notify those at the bottom that you are not going to be attending.

WAITING LISTS—ACCEPTED (SORT OF)

If you end up on the waiting list of a school or *the* school at the top of the list, you'll understand how important an early withdrawal notification is because you won't know if you will be going there until someone else rejects the program. Waiting lists are very frustrating for everyone involved. If it is for a school you especially hoped to attend, it is important to find out your position on the list relative to the length of it. If you are one of the top 10, your chances to be accepted are fairly good but still potentially iffy.

Waiting lists become especially tricky if you are also hoping for tuition breaks or loans administered through the school. If you are going to need financial help to go to that school, you need to talk to whoever administers the pool to find out if it is realistic to expect that kind of funding if you are admitted from the waiting list. Knowing can help you decide if you want to stay on the list and accept your next best choice as a contingency or just drop off the list and let someone else move into the slot.

ACCEPTED BY ONE AND WAITING FOR ALL

Some schools will let you defer acceptance for a few weeks. It may be that you are uncertain whether you want to go where you've been accepted, and you haven't yet heard whether you'll be accepted by the school at the top of your list. Call the admissions office to find out how long you can delay responding. Please note: We are not suggesting that you call up to ask *if* you can delay accepting, we are recommending that you push them for a deadline extension. Be diplomatic. They don't want to hear that they are your fallback school and you want to hear from somewhere else before deciding. You can always indicate that you are waiting to hear about possible funding or that you are uncertain about some personal matter that should be resolved within a few weeks. Be sure to express how thrilled you were to be accepted and that you hope they can accommodate you for a few weeks. Make sure you get the name and the correct spelling of the person who gives you an adjusted deadline. Then, send a letter of acknowledgment and confirmation of the agreed-to dates in the next-day mail. You must honor the date you agreed to by calling to notify them of your decision and immediately send a follow-up letter. Remember the caveat about the programs being like small towns.

WANT TO GO BUT CAN'T GO

If it turns out that something has happened between the application process and the letter of acceptance that forces you to delay going to school, contact the school immediately. A number of schools will allow you to defer your admission for 1 year and still retain your status as an accepted applicant. The most common reasons for deferring are pregnancy (it is very hard to get through a pregnancy and school at the same time), illness (yours or a close family member), changes in economic circumstances and job security, natural disasters, accidents, and family problems. All of these are generally considered legitimate reasons for delaying admission, and most schools have at least a few students annually that defer for a year.

If you find that you want to defer for reasons that are vague (the cold feet syndrome), or because you've decided you'd rather travel around for awhile, don't expect the school to be sympathetic. As much as we hate to admit it, universities are becoming more like businesses. They expect people to show up when they are supposed to show up and finish when they are supposed to finish. Like most corporations, they base their workloads on what they think their class sizes and student flow will be and are not sympathetic to students who don't seem committed to coming in and getting out in a timely manner.

Some students we talked to admitted that they deferred admission for 1 year at another school. They considered it a way of keeping open options in case the school they attended wasn't what they hoped it would be. The reality may differ tremendously from the expectation, and you might decide that you need (or want) to go somewhere else after the first year. This can be a bit tricky. You have to be clear that you are hoping to transfer in after a year and that you are going to be taking courses at another school. The school may or may not go along with your plan. If they don't, you might be starting over when you transfer to the other school.

If you decide to stay where you are, you *must* notify any school with which you have a delayed admission that you will not be attending. If you don't, you will be effectively denying another student admission because you will be in that slot.

ACCEPTANCE AND CERTAINTY

Many women get into the school at the top of their list and are thrilled. Our advice is, send in the letter of acceptance the moment you know for certain that's where you want to go. Then celebrate. This is an exciting and important moment, and we encourage you to celebrate joyously your coming adventures.

DISABILITIES AND SCHOOL CHOICES

If you have a disability and need special accommodations, it important to determine before accepting if the school actually can meet your needs. One school assured a student in a wheelchair that the campus was fully accessible. However, when winter came, she found out that curb cuts were where they generally dumped the snow, making it impossible for her to attend classes most of the academic year. In addition, the parking spaces for the disabled had no relationship to the locations of curb cuts or doors and many of the power-assisted doors did not work during the winter months because the mechanisms froze. She often found herself wheeling down a busy street looking for a way to get onto the sidewalk and waiting for someone to open doors for her. The fact that the campus buildings were connected by raised and covered walkways had seemed to her a good indication of the accessibility of the campus. However, she was unable to get onto campus most days, and when she attempted to withdraw and get a refund, the school balked and insisted that there was no problem.

The message here is, if the person telling you the campus is accessible is not disabled, they don't know. Find out from someone with a disability comparable to your own how you are going to fare in that environment, and then decide if it is or isn't a good place for you to pursue a degree.

Some disabilities may require status reviews postacceptance. This is most likely to apply to students who are undergoing active treatment for a major medical or psychiatric condition or who have indicated that they may need to take a leave of absence. They allow the school to stop the clock to prevent problems with completion of degree within a prescribed time line.

BEING REJECTED—ALTERNATIVES

Anyone who has opened a letter that begins, "We are sorry to inform you . . . " is likely to experience the immediate crush of frustration, anger, disappointment, and sadness. Many people find the condolence line of "We received many applications from fine applicants like yourself . . . " supremely irritating and not consoling in the slightest. It is strange how being rejected by a school can enhance its desirability. In addition, if the first letter you receive is a letter of rejection, it is likely that you will also experience a sense of impending doom about your likelihood of getting into any school. Hopefully the planning you did in Chapters 1 and 2 should prevent this from occurring.

It is not advisable to contact the school that rejected you with the just-opened letter is still in hand. You need time to formulate a discussion strategy that will work for you either emotionally or professionally or both. Blasting the director of admissions (or whomever signed the letter), or worse, the admissions clerk, is tempting but cannot be justified. It is unprofessional; it is emotionally unsatisfying; it can return to haunt you; and it will certainly limit future opportunities at that institution.

WHEN A REJECTION IS NOT A REJECTION

Sometimes, a school will notify an applicant that they are not accepted because they have failed to meet specific program requirements. This usually concerns mandatory prerequisites for admission to a program based on standards or courses that an accrediting body requires (see Chapter 2). When a program establishes a prerequisite, it is because they have discovered that successful students have basic knowledge and skills in a particular area. There is no point in arguing with the requirements. However, if you feel that a course you have taken covers the same material but the course title doesn't make that clear, there are ways to address the issue proactively.

> Lonzena's letter indicated that her application would be reconsidered once she met the prerequisites for the program. She was told that without a course in prealgebra, she could not be admitted. Her undergraduate degree, which was conferred in Jamaica, included a minor in physics. After making an appointment with the chair of the mathematics department, she pulled an advanced calculus text from his bookshelf and requested he select two problems for her to solve. While he watched, she successfully solved the problems. She asked him to contact the academic dean of the MBA program and advise

him of her competency in calculus. Happy to do so, he also tried to
recruit her into the mathematics department because he was im-
pressed with the elegance of her solution. The prerequisite was
waived and she was admitted.

Lonzena developed a creative solution to her problem. She correctly assessed that the prerequisite was a skills issue, and she needed
to demonstrate skills in that area. She found an expert that the business
school would respect, demonstrated the skill, and then used him as an
advocate within the system.

Find out exactly what it is that you need to do to reverse the
conditional status. If it involves course work, determine if you can
take the course in any accredited university or college. If you take it
in another university, be sure to get it preapproved by submitting a
copy of the course syllabus to the department and request confirmation of approval in writing. Be sure to clarify whether the course can
be taken concurrently to entry into the program or if you will need
proof of completion to begin.

Determine if the grade you receive affects your standing as a
conditional acceptee. Determine the minimum grade acceptable to
meet the requirement. Don't shoot for that grade, but if the course is
a horror and you only need a C in it to get accepted, then strive for a
B (if your mother is reading this, we meant an A).

FINDING OUT WHAT WENT WRONG

If you expected to be accepted and weren't, then it may be to your
advantage to find out what went wrong. Before you assume that the
problem is with you, it is important to find out exactly what happened.
It could be something as simple as a reference letter not getting to the
school in time, and you were rejected for an incomplete package.
Likewise, your paperwork may not have been received in time, even
though you mailed it in 3 weeks before the deadline. These things are
not entirely under your control, but they affected you adversely and
can leave you feeling somehow at fault.

If it turns out that the problem was with the timeliness of a
reference letter, you need to be careful about using that person again
where time lines matter. They may have great things to say about you,
but if they cannot be counted on to respond in a timely manner, then

it doesn't really matter. If the problem is that you live in an area where weather can compromise mail delivery (snow, rain, hail, sleet aside), then it may be worth using a courier service or planning to get material in 2-3 weeks ahead of the deadline. Couriers are more efficient but more expensive.

If you can substantiate that you had every reason to expect the school to have a complete package in a timely manner, ascertain if they will consider you for a waiting list position. It is certainly worth talking to someone about, but understand that it is unlikely that the admissions clerk is the one to engage in the discussion. She may, however, point you to the right person, so don't argue with her. Furthermore, she may well understand what the most appealing arguments would be, so do get her advice. People tend to overlook how much the support staff people know about the system and how best to manipulate it.

Some schools allow you to use the same application the next year without resubmitting and without reincurring admission costs. If this school continues to be your first or only choice, it is worth finding out whether you'll have to reapply or not. It is important that you know how close you were to being accepted based on your application, your grades, and graduate examination scores before you exercise this option. If you were substantially below the cut for the waiting list, then this is the time to reevaluate either your goals or your choice in schools.

If you were rejected by all schools, there are a series of steps you need to take. First, you need to reevaluate the match between your goals and the profession or graduate programs you selected. It may be that you are not fundamentally suited for the degree you seek. It may also be that you have misunderstood what the degree you are seeking will actually prepare you to do, and nothing in your package provided the schools with any validation that you are a good candidate. It may also be that your past educational achievements are poor and that you are not competitive as a result. You may perceive part of the problem to be grade inflation in the current academic climate. Although that may be a realistic concern, there isn't much you can do about it, and theoretically, the graduate examination scores should help to compensate for your grade point average.

If you can't figure out what went wrong, it is advisable to talk to the appropriate admissions person in the school you selected as your fallback school, if possible. It is not something that could or even should be discussed on the telephone. Schools are concerned about potential violations of your confidentiality if the person cannot document that they spoke with you, and it is very difficult to produce identification over the telephone.

Understand that there are legitimate limitations to the information you will be provided. The school's representative may not tell you the content in your letters of reference if the persons writing the letters invoked confidentiality. In the same way, if they had serious problems with things you said in the interview, you may only be told that you seemed unsuited for the program and or profession without further elaboration. You may also be told that your essay wasn't up to standards, but you may not get details about what the specific problems were because that might constitute coaching you for your next try.

Do try to find out if it was the whole package or a particular part of the package that was a problem. It might be possible to increase your graduate examination scores, take courses to upgrade your grade point average, or to rewrite your essay. Once you've gotten general information about where the problem or problems lie, then it is up to you to discern what is an appropriate adjustment or change.

Your references may have been the problem. Either the people writing them qualified their recommendations, or you had people who did not provide information salient to your academic and career goals. You might want to consider requesting different people to write letters for you. Your overall package may be improved by getting employment or doing volunteer work in a related field (remember, these are good references).

PROVING YOUR WORTH AND ABILITIES

One sure way to improve your status as an applicant is to take any electives you can in the program as a nonmatriculating student and then use that faculty member as a reference. Next best is to take courses as a nonmatriculating student in a similar but different department at the same university, and use that faculty member as a reference. These courses must be at the graduate level and fairly rigorous. Keep in mind that if you do poorly on these courses, it may be that graduate schools have correctly evaluated your potential to succeed in that discipline.

Finding employment in a related field is also a possible way of evaluating your potential in the field. If you work for someone with a graduate degree, they might be in a position to advocate for your candidacy. However, if your undergraduate grades are low and your examination scores are poor, no amount of advocacy will work. Your ability to do graduate-level academics will remain in question.

REJECTING THEM

Before you go to all of this trouble, be certain that it matters to you to know exactly what the problem is rather than responding to the rejection. If, however, it turns out that all of the schools turned you down, then the question is more likely whether you selected the appropriate field for you rather than the right schools. It may be time to reevaluate your goals and the match of field to those goals.

It also may be that you have a fatal flaw in your package. Regardless of how good your essay, work history, and references are, a low grade point average and low graduate examination scores may exclude you from serious consideration in most graduate programs. If you continue to want the degree, then establish academic credibility by going back to school and cleaning up your undergraduate record.

It may be that you, like Gloria, decided on a major without adequately evaluating what the current demands are in that field. If, like Gloria, you think you want to go into developmental psychology but, unlike Gloria, despise mathematics, the low C's and D's you got in basic logic and algebra may be excluding you because the current demands of the profession are math intensive.

SUMMARY

The process of waiting to find out if you got into graduate school is stressful. There are advantages to rank ordering schools before the letters start coming in.

Decisions should be made based on your goals and what schools have to offer you in achieving those goals. Some may offer a more elite or rigorous academic environment, but they may not be scholarship rich or may have workloads that exceed your available time.

It is likely that a school may reject you. There are times when you should just blow it off and times when it is important to determine what went wrong. It is best to formulate a plan about who to talk to and what to ask before you call the school.

Last, celebrate the acceptance letters as they arrive. It is the first step of an exciting journey, and the moment should be savored. The next time you will be this elated is at graduation.

5

PAYING FOR IT

In this chapter, we discuss the financial realities of graduate school and make some suggestions about how you can make ends meet. We talk about the resources available on-line to locate scholarships and loans and how to track down funds targeted for your area of study. We also look at some of the hidden costs in attending universities and how you can negotiate around some of them.

FINANCIAL REALITIES

One of the main hurdles that women face in graduate school is that they can experience greater economic disadvantages than their male counterparts. They are likely to have earned less, saved less, and have fewer economic resources available. So the question becomes, Who's got the money and how can I get some?

There are a number of steps that should be considered in assessing how bad or good your financial picture is before you start looking for loans. The 11 steps include the following:

1. Determine how much money you will need monthly and over the course of the degree, accounting for inflation at a minimum rate of 7%.

2. Determine your financial assets and liabilities against your current and potential earnings during the school year and factor in differential earnings during summers and breaks.

3. Determine what nonacademic expenses and obligations are fixed and what can be cut, deferred, transferred, or refused.

4. Determine the feasibility and likelihood of finding part-time employment while in school (full-time during breaks and summers).

5. Determine tolerable adjustments to your own and your family's standards of living.

6. Determine how much of a loan burden you can carry after graduate school.

7. Apply for any reasonable assistantship.

8. Apply for general scholarships.

9. Apply to community groups that offer appropriate scholarships.

10. Apply for all relevant university scholarships.

11. Make up the balance with loans.

Once you've walked yourself through this list (and we will walk you through most of it in greater detail), you need to ask yourself a fundamental question: Is it economically doable at this time to attend graduate school? Remember that you may have the option to defer your entry into a program for a year while you earn and set aside additional income, so we recommend that you tackle the issues in this chapter simultaneous to your acceptance into a program or programs. Of course, we also recommend celebrating first.

HOW MUCH DO YOU REALLY NEED?

It is difficult to anticipate all of the economic contingencies that you are likely to face during a graduate education. Regardless of what you think your bottom line will be, you will probably need another 20% to cover all the associated costs and unexpected expenditures. Tuition costs have a way of increasing, as do those for books and other supplies. Unpredictable expenses have a way of occurring when you feel least able to handle them. Our experience is that too many students harbor an optimism that if the figures appear to be in waving distance of each other, providence will provide for the rest. Although faith and good fortune may carry you through some rough spots, it is foolish to count on it entirely. This is not the time to say, "I just know that things will work out; they always do."

Graduate education has enough stresses attached to it without finding yourself unable to cope economically and possibly emotionally with impending financial disasters, particularly in very challenging and demanding disciplines. Realistically, the cost of school can drain financial reserves and earning power to the point of potential evictions, bankruptcy, and family dissolution. As one bursar put it, "In the universe we trust; at the university we expect money."

DEVELOPING A BOTTOM LINE

It is easier to envision all of this if you are going to be staying where you are—same home, same community, same relationships, same job, and same bills. There are clear economic advantages to doing so as long as the school matches your goals and objectives; you can afford the tuition, books, and supplies; and you have a job that won't compete for the time that you need to complete the program. However, if you are already living in one of the 10 most expensive cities in the country and planning to attend a school with hefty tuition, then you might want to revisit Chapter 2 and reevaluate the advantages to considering schools out of town.

Table 5.1 can get you started in calculating financial resources. Draw up a similar one for your debts and set expenses. Regardless of whether you are moving or staying, you need to anticipate now that your credit card debt will probably skyrocket. It is best to beat it down as close as you can to a zero balance before you embark on a graduate program.

COSTS ASSOCIATED WITH RELOCATING

In addition to those fixed expenses and income sources, relocation has an immediate impact on any budget. There are a number of costs that you need to consider.

Table 5.1   Monthly Income Work Sheet

Savings/interest	_____
Employment	_____
Loans	_____
Scholarships/bursaries	_____
Family/friend contributions	_____
Organizational support(s)	_____
Employer reimbursements	_____
Child support	_____
Disability/retraining monies	_____
Welfare/family benefits	_____
Pensions/retirement	_____
Fellowships	_____
Graduate assistantship	_____
Other	_____
Total	_____

Clothing

Clothing expenditures are obvious if you are relocating. Most women who relocate don't find themselves in the same climate. Whether you love clothing or are a basic jeans and T-shirt or sweatshirt person, relocation often requires clothing additions. It is important to also keep in mind that some programs have explicit or implicit dress standards (see Chapter 8).

Do not head off on a buying trip to the mall before you get to the new community. It is important to wait until you figure out how students generally dress and decide whether you want to be identified as idiosyncratic by your dress. It may be possible to achieve creative alternatives to a new wardrobe and still maintain an acceptable image.

If your financial picture is marginal, there are advantages to purchasing clothing in a second-hand store in your new location. Consignment shops provide climate-appropriate clothing and generally reflect the local styles. Regardless, if you move to a colder climate, you will have to invest in boots, coats, hats, scarves, gloves—all fairly high-ticket items. Buy the best you can afford, and buy as neutral as you can stand for longer and more flexible wear. If you move to a much warmer climate, you may find that the fabrics you've been wearing in Alberta are going to make you miserable in Southern California.

To get an idea of what a climate-appropriate wardrobe of basic items is going to run, get standard catalogs sent to you (e.g., Lands' End, Eddie Bauer, L. L. Bean) and compare prices. Winter coats are now coded with comfort indexes so you'll know if it is going to keep you warm in –70 degree weather. If you're reading this section, we doubt we need to say anything about focusing on sale items. Remember, winter clothing sale prices start in February or March and summer sales start in June or July.

▓ Moving and Other Nightmares

Attached to moving are new housing costs, including nonrefundable key money (where you buy an existing lease or the opportunity to rent—common in large metropolitan areas), first and last month deposits, security, and utility connections (often including a hefty deposit if it is a new account). Many apartments do not provide shades for windows, so buying shades or the ever-popular sheets need to be factored in.

In some communities, parking your car can add substantially to monthly expenses, so either plan for this cost or sell the car. Selling your car is especially appealing if you plan on living near public transportation (obviously, more applicable in large cities) or near enough to the school to ride the campus transportation system, if there is one.

If you are going to relocate, you need to get to the new community early enough not to compete with students who descend 2 or 3 weeks before classes commence. We suggest July as opposed to August, if possible. In addition, if you are planning on doing part-time work, it is easier to find employment during the summer than when everyone arrives. In a perfect world, you can plan to find a cheap apartment that is located midway between work and campus but far away from students who party all night long (unless you have an additional social agenda in mind). The earlier you show up, the more likely you will find paradise.

Moving expenses vary but the basic formula is simple: The less stuff you move, the less it will cost. So if you are going to be moving, begin by getting rid of as much as you can. Purge, purge, purge your closets, kitchen cabinets, book cases, knickknacks, and anything else you don't have a deep sentimental attachment to or will actually need.

If you can't stand purging, loan items to people who can use them while you go to school. Remember, this is the time to find a buyer for that frilly, gilded, and atrocious china your grandmother willed to you and you've never put on the table. Think of it this way: She will help you pay for your education—a wonderful legacy.

The next decision you have to make is whether to move yourself and whether to do it with or without a rental truck. The self-move can reduce but not eliminate the costs of moving. Consider the potential back injuries you can incur while attempting to get the couch on the truck. So if you are planning to do the heavy work, get help. That's what friends and families are for. Renting a truck is feasible if you are going some distance (over 200 miles, or 330 kilometers), although you may get some annoying gender-laden comments from the guy renting you the truck if it is bigger than a van. So decide in advance how you are going to handle the "does the little lady have someone to help her" attitude and comments. It could be awkward to have to explain your requested admission delay to fight assault charges.

Professional movers are expensive. They charge by the hour or by the pound and mileage if you move more than a few miles. Here are the things you won't get from the glossy brochures that make moving look like a "fun" and "effortless" adventure. You can cut costs if you pack most of the things yourself and use as many boxes of a uniform size as you can find. Get cartons from the mover: The uniformity of size makes loading the truck faster; you will have less damage; and if the driver sees cartons from the carrier, he or she tends to assume the carrier packed it and is liable for damages (drivers pay for damages). Get an estimate for the move with and without packing and with and without boxes. If you can afford it, have them pack the breakables unless you take time to learn how to do it right. Pack your own books, tapes, CDs, and records; pack clothing in plastic baggies and leave them in the bureau drawers (they then don't have to be unpacked and stay clean). Clothing can be packed in wardrobe boxes from the carrier (pack tightly to avoid wrinkles, pin clothing to hangers to avoid slippage to the bottom, and place clothing inside plastic dry-cleaning bags for smoother and tighter fit). Use pillows, blankets, bedding, and towels around important fragile valuables to keep them safe. Of course, take a set of sheets, pillows, pillow cases, towels, a shower curtain and hooks, and shampoo and soap with you in the car, so when they unpack the bed, you can shower and have someplace clean to sleep that night. Also, take the coffee pot, coffee, and cups with you—you'll need them (put sugar in a jar and get boxed milk).

The driver is usually obligated to unpack three things if you cross state lines. Have him set up the heavy furniture, so decide exactly where it goes in advance. Drivers are notoriously impatient and cranky people unless you flash that $20.00 tip early. Buy the insurance without deduction. A $250 deductible represents a lot of damage, and if the driver knows there is no deductible, he or she has no leeway on damages and is likely to be more careful. Be sure to find out what the driver likes to drink (nonalcoholic, of course); have plenty of it and ice on hand at both ends, with plastic glasses. Loading and unloading a truck is hard work, and if the driver thinks you're taking care of him or her, then you have a better chance of the driver taking care of you.

Cars

Next, you need to consider the cost of supporting a car where you are going. Obviously, the costs of registering, insuring, and housing cars vary tremendously from place to place. If you move from one country to another (e.g., United States to or from Canada) be careful that you don't inadvertently violate laws regarding registering your car. The fines can be heavy. Find out what you can do to reduce insurance costs. It might be cheaper, for instance, to rent a garage than pay insurance for on-the-street parking. In addition, different climates demand different features in cars. A car that runs great in a flat and warm climate can be a disaster in a mountainous and snowy locale. Worse, you may find yourself unable to sell your semi-useless car (especially in winter months) and still end up paying for registration, parking, and insurance. In some climates, it is advisable to consider waxing and otherwise treating your car if you plan on having it for more than 1 year. If, on the other hand, you buy clunkers, drive them into the ground, and buy another one, then waxing is a waste of time.

Computers

Most women understand that a distinguishing characteristic of graduate education is the large number of papers and reports you will be writing. As computers become more commonplace, faculty members become less tolerant of typographical errors, misspellings, and poor grammar, especially as software programs are now equipped with spelling and grammar checks. Faculty members expect students to turn in papers that resemble professional-looking reports complete with tables and graphics as appropriate. The question is not whether you should use a computer, but whose computer should you use.

Some schools have adequate student computing facilities. If yours has computing resources, find out if the student computers are generally available or have very restricted hours or long waiting lines. Also determine how many sites are on campus relative to its size, what kinds of printers are available, and whether you have to buy your own diskettes. If the school has good computer resources, the programs you need, hours that work for you, and excellent printers, then you never have to worry about computer problems. Best of all, if the computer you're on isn't working, you just move over to the next system.

Before we go any further, an obvious word of warning about diskettes. *Never* put diskettes that have been used on student computers in your own computer. Get color-coded diskettes so you always know where the diskette came from before putting it in your A drive. It is possible you will be loading a software virus with the disc, and the potential hassles that follow are not worth the risks. If you must swap diskettes with other students, get a virus protection program, and *always* check a diskette for viruses before using it.

There is a growing trend on many campuses that students must have their own personal computers—which is their way of saying that students can no longer expect the university to provide this resource. Universities find it difficult and expensive to keep current with personal computing hardware and software and would prefer to spend those dollars elsewhere.

Let's assume that the school you're attending has adopted the philosophy that students should have their own systems. It is not necessary to arrive at school with a computer ready to plug in if you are relocating. Moving a computer is risky. All kinds of things can go wrong, and you'll end up fighting with the movers (if you're using one) about whose fault it is or furious with yourself (if you aren't using a professional mover) when your system crashes because of that crater-sized pot hole that also destroyed your axle. If you are going to move a system, try to find the original packing materials or see if you can get some from a computer store. In other words, slow down, observe, ask questions, and wait before investing thousands of dollars in a system.

The reality is that you won't know what kind of a system or what sorts of programs you are going to need until you start attending classes. Computer stores have a vested interest in exploiting your enthusiasm (and with it, your wallet) by selling you the biggest and the best system they have. It may turn out that most of the time, you are going to be doing word processing, not desk-top publishing or complex statistical analysis with your personal computer. Waiting is especially important if you have already hemorrhaged most of your savings on moving costs and tuition.

Remember that computers are expensive and that they have a way of becoming obsolete within a few years. The more scientific and mathematical your field is, the more memory you must have to handle these programs. Memory is expensive and so are the programs needed to access and present data. Because cost issues are so important, keep in mind that university bookstores often get student discount programs intended for academic environments, which may not be available in the large computer discount stores. So before you run off to a computer store with your letter of acceptance in hand, it is best think through some salient issues first.

You may have to buy one almost as soon as you arrive. Most schools have competitive microcomputer stores or sections in the bookstore. Find a peer expert (or a peer's kid who's an expert) to go shopping with you if you don't know your baud from your RAM. It is advisable to do this before you get to the computer store. This way, you can walk in with specifications in hand and order a system that will meet your needs without having to engage in techno-jargon with some kid that can't translate any of it into intelligible English.

The best information source for the kind of system that you'll need are women who are a year ahead of you in the program. They have the best and most accurate idea of what your needs are going to be in the first semester. If it turns out that all of your first-semester course grades are going to be based on tests and examinations, a computer isn't going to be particularly useful or necessary. Then, you can shop around during semester (or quarter) break for a system tailored to your needs.

If you can't find a peer or a peer's kid who is a techno-freak, realize that universities have experts in their computing and information technology centers. These are usually the same people who run the help desks. It is worth getting to know one of them well enough to ask him or her to write down what systems are currently a good value. Because many of these systems can be seen on the internet and purchased by mail, they will also help you figure out how to order the system. In all probability, that is where they are getting their personal computers from, and they are usually more than happy to tell you what and how to order. Just make clear what your demands will be and what you can reasonably spend. It may be possible for them to provide you with specifications to then match to a catalog.

If you have never set up a computer, it can be quite a challenge. If you are a computer ignoramus, it might be worth paying them a consultant fee to design, order, and then set up the system. Often, they will spend time customizing the system so that you can click into the programs you commonly use without a lot of steps, set up some basic files for you, and show you how to get around within the system easily.

It is unlikely that you will be spending much less than $2,000 if you buy a very basic new system. If you buy a used system, be sure you have the system checked out by a techno-freak so that you don't buy one that is either too limited, incompatible with the university systems, too slow, or has a virus that causes the system to crash continuously.

It is neither advisable nor useful for us to recommend an all-purpose system. The reliability of systems change with each model, and some companies change the model multiple times during the year. Programs are also difficult to recommend because they change with the available technology and the latest "hot" programs.

Understand that learning how to use a computer or a new operating system or even a more recent version of a familiar program has substantial learning curves attached. It can be very frustrating to learn apparently simple things, such as opening, naming, closing, saving, and merging files. If you are just starting on a computer, don't assume that it is like a typewriter that you can plug in and start generating a paper.

If possible, defer the expense and learning curve for a semester or two until you've gotten settled into the environment. Once you are settled in, taking on the experience of becoming more or less computer literate will be more effective. There are some wonderful *Dummies* texts by the IDG Books Worldwide Company (Foster City, CA) that provide information on how to get around in most of the word processing and internet programs. They have figured out how real people ask "how-to" questions and then answered them in straightforward ways. It makes it possible to cut down the frustrations associated with the learning curve, and more important, it cuts down on idiosyncratic and ineffectual ways of using programs. These books are generally available in computer stores, university bookstores, and most regular bookstores with a computer section.

If you can't find someone willing to teach you or can't find the *Dummies* series, then sign up for a computer course in the program you are trying to learn. There are usually courses available on campus on how to use various word processing programs and statistical analysis packages taught by user- friendly folks. Over time, you'll find that most people learn the tricks and short cuts from each other. Generally, very confusing information can be found in the manuals provided by the operating system and the programs you bought for your computer. They tend to assume that you know what you are looking at and for, are fluent in computerese, understand how they define functions, and are just looking for a reminder. Some people in the business believe that the least talented or useful member of the product development team is the one assigned to write the manuals. In other words, for many people, the manuals rest unopened on a shelf until they become obsolete.

What we don't recommend is using a typist. They don't care as much as you do about the quality or the precision of the work. They are expensive because they tend to charge by the page, and revisions are as expensive as a first-run paper. In reality, typists are becoming obsolete. Of course, if you won the lottery, have lots of money, and hate typing, by all means, help support some desperate graduate student with a computer and time to spare.

WHO'S GOT THE MONEY AND HOW DO I GET SOME?

Relatives and Friends

The first line of support for many women going on or going back to school are their friends and families. We'd like to take this opportunity to thank all of those wonderful people who cooked meals, provided free babysitting, did chores, gave clothing and household furnishings, provided cash, edited papers, and encouraged us to succeed. Without you, this would have been much tougher to do.

Working and Surviving

For many women, graduate school costs require them to find employment with sufficient flexibility that they can tinker with the schedule each semester (or quarter) to accommodate their class schedules. The women that we interviewed across the country, in a wide variety of disciplines, recommend that you find essentially mindless work to do. The jobs most commonly suggested were sales clerks, cashiers, waitressing, clerical support, receptionists, and telephone sales. One of the more ideal places to look for work is on campus in one of the departments (preferably not your own) as a staff support person. Such positions may carry with them tuition waivers or reductions. If it is a decent school, they will allow you flex time to help you meet the challenges of the ever-changing schedule.

If you need a higher-paying position, keep in mind that there are some liabilities attached. Many of the women we talked to who kept professional-level, higher paying jobs found that the stresses of school *and* work tended to be significant, especially because they often had household responsibilities to keep up with as well. We were surprised by the number of women who said that if they had it to do over, they would have lowered their standard of living in the short run. They felt that they were often fragmented by conflicting demands on their time and energies. In the long run, some felt that they didn't get the grades they could have gotten, and that made them less competitive when they started hunting for work after they graduated. A number also commented that their employers in higher paying professional jobs treated graduate school as a luxury and were very unsympathetic about academic demands impinging on work productivity. The recurrent theme is that mindless work is the best and that it is work that you leave behind mentally as you punch out for the day.

There still are the rare employers who fully support graduate work and work to accommodate ever-changing schedules. They may pay all or part of tuition costs. Some even pick up the cost of fees, books, and supplies. They reasonably expect you to pay them back by agreeing to a long-term commitment in exchange for these benefits. The alternative is to find something at a university and college. They figure that they can underpay you while you are going to school because they often waive tuition or give significant tuition reductions. If you become a long-term employee, they may also extend these benefits to your children, at least through undergraduate education. The benefits tend to diminish at the upper and professional degrees.

Keep in mind that some employers will demand reimbursement for the educational benefits proportionate to the unmet commitment. If you are being supported by your employer, be sure to find out whether it is possible to pay off any of the benefits concurrently, such as during the summer or between semesters when you can shift to full-time work. Also, determine if you can get partial support and incur a shorter obligation period. One of the things that people often fail to clarify is whether there will be any promotional advantages to getting the advanced degree. It is very frustrating to work for an organization at the same level with the same pay after completing a grueling graduate program and know you are stuck there for a few years. "They like to have female MBA's around, but they don't like to move us into upper management positions where we can do what we were trained to do," said one women we talked to about her experience with tuition reimbursement.

Fellowships and Graduate Assistantships

Many schools have fellowships available to graduate students. Unfortunately, they are limited, so when you first start putting your financial picture together and it is clear you're going to need financial help, explore whether fellowships and assistantships are offered in the programs to which you have applied. These are funds you do not have to repay, but you will have to work for the money. Fellowships are often attached to research projects and are part of the funded studies, so if you get one, you will be doing a lot of grunt work to help support the study. In some fields, this includes such exciting work as cleaning the cages of the laboratory animals, pulling and copying journal articles, picking up and delivering data computer runs, coding and doing data entry, proofing documents, collecting data (usually the most undesirable data, of course), or typing and collating reports. One of us had the unpleasant task of "cleaning up" manuscripts for publication that bordered on illiterate gibberish, for a few dollars a week. It may sound glamorous when you are applying, but do get details before you agree. You may either hate the tasks or be unable to do the work they have targeted with the fellowship funds.

Assistantships are usually connected to a faculty or school rather than to a project. What you do as a graduate assistant varies by school, though in many cases, it is likely to be broken down by gender lines unless you are in a field where women are not a minority. It seems as if female graduate assistants in some programs pick up the clerical work, whereas males tend to do library work and other so-called research-oriented work. Some schools also use assistants as adjuncts in the classroom for such exciting tasks as starting and stopping videos, passing out material, gathering assignments from students, or taking attendance.

Gender discrimination in assistantships or fellowships is frustrating and grossly unfair and, hopefully, is becoming less common. In your first year, you would be most likely to be assigned as an assistant to faculty members who are the least sensitive and supportive of equity among men and women. Unfortunately, complaining is not likely to get you reassigned to a more appropriate and intelligent faculty person. The reason you got that assignment is because the second-year women fellows already know about this bozo. Worse, other faculty people may covertly acknowledge that this kind of discrimination is going on but feel helpless to intervene. Wanting to pursue it is understandable and potentially politically satisfying. It will also cost you a great deal of time and money, and it will probably result in the loss of the fellowship or assistantship for that year. It can be an entrenched system, so your best shot is to try to get reassigned to a sensitive female or male faculty member the second year who will remember his or her own resentment of the arcane system and treat you as a competent and intelligent person.

Sexual harassment, of course, is never acceptable and should never be tolerated. You shouldn't have to make clear your boundaries in the first place, but if you have and the behavior continues, it becomes a reportable offense. You are justified in expecting the school to respond to the offensive behavior for what it is and take the appropriate actions. Most departments or institutions in graduate education have formal policies to deal with sexual harassment issues. Check those out first and follow them as seems appropriate. Alternatively, begin with the program director or the dean of the school and discuss what happened candidly and openly. However, most of us know horror stories where sexual harassment has been minimized or trivialized or where the woman reporting it has been harassed in other ways. If that happens, the National Organization for Women (NOW) can help you deal with the situation effectively, and they are worth contacting. If you are lucky enough to have a law clinic in town or connected to the university, it may be possible to get some legal advice about how to proceed.

Scholarships and Loans

Planning early for scholarships and loans is important if fellow-ships and assistantships aren't available. Therefore, we address how to identify sources for these monies first. There are a surprising number of loans, scholarships, bursaries, and organizations that can provide financial support while you go to school, even in financially conservative times. The question is how to find out where the monies are and what you have to do to get some before others do.

Many women assume that scholarships and loans are tied to academic excellence. In reality, there are numerous scholarships that are tied to professional goals. In addition, some are tied to helping women gain entry into fields not generally identified with women or fields that are waning in popularity for women, to encourage them to select the field. If you are thinking of applying for funds that are goal oriented or professionally oriented, you need to revisit Chapter 1 and decide how to shape those goals into a form that will be financially advantageous to you without selling out.

Also, if you know you are going to have to rely heavily on external funding, scholarships are better than loans. When you begin looking at possible schools (Chapter 2), make sure that you talk to the financial aid offices to determine the amount of annual scholarships at the institution and what student populations are the biggest beneficiaries. Some schools are richer in scholarships than others. They recognize that they cannot attract a broad variety of students without some financial support and make scholarships available based on need rather than academic superiority.

A fairly reliable source for current general scholarship and loan information can be gotten from the Internet. Using "http://www.search.com" (and if you don't know what this is, ask any kid for a tour of the internet), you can key on to the education directory and then enter "educational loans" to get the most current listing of loan directories. When we wrote this, it was possible to get information about how to consolidate loans, loans available through the U.S. federal government, a direct loan newsletter, student guides to loans, loans targeting minorities, loan deferment regulations, campus-based programs, and so on. In other words, this search function will give you an idea of what kinds of loans are available to students across disciplines. More important, it will open avenues of information that you might not know exist.

There are additional on-line financial aid listings available at this time. For example, http://www.finaid.org, which is sponsored by the National Association of Financial Aid Administrators, will help you decide if a firm you've hired to search for scholarship funds has a good reputation (there are lots of fraudulent search firms out there, so be wary). Another one is http://www.nasfaa.org, which provides tips on how to apply for scholarships. The College Board now has a website (http://www.collegeboard.org) with a resource they call "Expand

Scholarship Search," which is available to college loan officers. It is a guide to scholarships out there that you might be eligible for and are worth checking out. Then, there is the http://salliemae.com, a home page that has scholarship and student loan information for browsing. Some of these charge you for the information, so be careful about incurring unexpected charges. If they ask for a credit card number, you will be billed for the service. A free service is found on http://www.rams.com/srn/search.htm that gets you into a whole network of information about loans available through the private sector.

There are a number of guidebooks on how to find and apply for loans. One of the best on private sector funds is by Daniel J. Cassidy (1996) titled, *The Scholarship Book* and published by Prentice Hall. One of the most expensive is put out by Brown and Benchmark Publishers and is titled *Financial Aid for Higher Education*. It is edited by Oreon Keeslar and comes with a hefty price tag. However, it provides a detailed listing of the criteria for over 3,000 sources of financial aid.

In the United States, organizations such as the Public Health Service, the Environmental Protection Agency, and the Department of Education have scholarships and fellowship funds available. You will wait at least 6 months before you know if you qualify for these scholarships, so plan well in advance and have a backup plan. In addition, even if you do qualify, it could take another 6 months before the check is made available to you. Do not consider these funds as being available during most of the first year (you could be evicted or starve before they are released). Many of the applications for these funds require a faculty sponsor. Until you become established, no one will know you well enough to write a letter of support or include you on a grant already funded.

Worse, these scholarships can be allocated but not funded. You may have been awarded one, only to find that the funding line has been cut and with it, your money. In that case, get in touch with your appropriate state representatives at both the House and Senate levels to complain. Remember that this strategy is only effective if you are still registered to vote in his or her area.

Each profession often has it's own student funding opportunities. To find out what kinds of scholarships or loans are available (especially to women), contact the professional licensing or educational headquarters for the profession, and ask for information. Many professions have funds targeted to support women, unless the field is already dominated by women. In addition, many professions are targeting people of diverse backgrounds for support, so if you identify with one of the groups generally considered a minority, it is worth contacting the professional organizations to find out whether there are any specific scholarships or loans that are appropriate for you. If you are targeting a particular institution, contact the alumni association to determine if they provide scholarships or if they are aware of scholarship or loan sources.

Many loans and scholarships are available only after the first year in the program. These tend to assume that people who aren't going to make it will wash out after the first year and so target "sure bets." Sure bet money is bigger but will also rely on faculty members' recommendations about how the applicant is expected to contribute to the field. To compete, faculty members need to know what you can do academically and what your career goals are. Sit down and discuss the funds you are applying for and what they need to include in the letters. Ask the faculty member if they would mind giving you a blind copy of the letter (meaning that they do not indicate that they have copied you on the letter) for your file. If the person states that they won't, then it might be worth reconsidering them as a reference. Disinclination to provide a blind copy suggests that the reference letter may not be as strong as you would hope for it to be.

In many communities, women's groups often will sponsor women going to graduate school—as long as it is for a degree or an area they endorse. They often don't care where you use the scholarship. These sources can usually be located by contacting national women's groups, women's organizations within professional associations, or women's societies within the community either where you currently live or those connected to the school. Remember that you are likely to be expected to make appearances at their meetings while you are in school and after graduation so that you can be showcased as "a local woman they helped to make good."

Many universities have remnants of faculty wives' clubs, which are usually called "university women's associations." They now generally have a split membership between an older group whose husbands were on faculty and a younger group of women faculty members. They almost always sponsor graduate and undergraduate scholarships for "promising young women." Even if the idea is galling, the amount of money can be worth a serious discussion with them and applying for the grant or loan. Remember, some of these monies are free (except for smiling for the camera and being shown off like a shar pei puppy), or if they come in the form of a loan, they are often interest free if they are paid back in a timely manner.

It is worth exploring the local resources as well. Universities may know what groups actively develop scholarships in the community.

Some groups may be small and not on the Internet, but bursaries and financial aid offices are aware of them either because the monies come into them directly or because students have promised payment as soon as their loan or grant monies are received.

A number of graduate students cobble together scholarships and loans to pay the costs of tuition, books, supplies, and partial living expenses. If this is your plan, start with scholarships (they are usually smaller amounts). Once you know what your scholarships will be, you can decide how much more in loans you'll need to get through an academic year.

Shop around to determine what group sponsors loans related to the particular degree you are pursuing. However, keep in mind that student loans have a way of not arriving when they were promised. It is advisable to have a backup plan. Until you have a sense of the cash flow, you are likely to be drawing from savings (or borrowing from friends and relatives), so we advise you to have at least the first 6 months' expenditure secured.

Bank Loans

Bank loans can be obtained quickly (at fairly decent interest rates) if you have a good credit rating and slowly (at exorbitant rates) if you have poor or no credit. Unlike student loans, whose repayment can be deferred until after graduation, bank loan repayment schedules begin immediately, the interest rates are higher, and some banks expect you to be employed and a good risk. It is not likely that they will consider you a desirable risk if you tell them that you are going to school full time, even if you are planning to work part time. Some banks are a little more lenient about the employment requirement, but you have to demonstrate that the degree you are pursuing guarantees employability at graduation and, of course, that you have a willing cosigner or assets. There are implicit, if not explicit, gender biases in who gets loans as a student from banks, with and without cosigners. In addition, banks tend to favor certain types of degrees more than others—not surprisingly, those more closely identified with "male" and "money-making" professions.

TUITION PAYMENTS

Deadlines are not always deadlines when it comes to the business or bursar's office. If you're lucky, all loans and scholarships will come in as monies are due. Of course, that isn't going to happen, and you're likely to be facing a month-to-month horror trying to get everything financially coordinated.

Dealing with the business office need not be adversarial. If possible, try to develop a relationship with a particular person in the office, and work with that person to achieve a mutually agreeable plan. This may include paying a weekly or monthly sum against the tuition balance after the loans come into the school. You must honor this agreement, and if you need to change or adjust it once it has been set, then do it formally. If the school sees you as a reliable payer, then they may occasionally overlook a late payment. However, if they perceive you as chronically late (which affects their cash flow balance), irritable, disrespectful, and unreliable, they are going to be inflexible about even the most mundane requests.

REPAYMENT OF LOANS

Many student loan repayment schedules are deferred until you have completed your program of study. This can include additional graduate work (an additional master's or a doctoral degree after completing a master's degree), though there are some time lines to discourage the perpetual student syndrome. Once the repayment schedule does start, penalties are substantial for late payments or payment default. In Canada, you can defer as long as you are in school, but repayment begins 6 months after graduation.

Do not get sloppy about payments. If you decide to go back for an additional degree and your repayment history isn't nearly perfect, you'll have a very hard time getting additional student loans. We very strongly recommend against defaulting on loans by filing bankruptcy. We know it is done. We think it is unconscionable to do so because you are effectively reducing the available funds for other students. You needed it—you got it; they need it—so pay up.

On the other hand, you may need to reduce the amount in the repayment schedule because of economic problems after graduation. Loans papers have information about who to contact to arrange for payment schedule adjustments. Understand that this will increase your interest burden on the loan. If you have no choice, then do it, and get the new payment agreement in writing.

■ Consolidating Loans

Student loans are often consolidated by the lender, though you may be able to consolidate your own loan burden into one monthly payment. Pay close attention to paperwork related to the loans as they come through, because you're not going to know who to make out the check to if your loans were consolidated by the lenders. If you send the payment to the wrong bank or financial institution, the holder of the note will consider your payment late or defaulted, and you will incur penalties. It's frustrating, and it happens all the time. You may or may not get a loan book from the new institution, so go through all banking mail sent to you carefully. What you think is advertisement may be information about the latest institution to buy your loan. One of us has paid off one loan to three different banking institutions in a 6-year period. The point of all of this is that loans, like mortgages, are often consolidated and sold. The changes must be kept track of to avoid problems—so read everything that appears to be an official bank document. Call if you aren't certain, because sometimes it appears as if it's a bank trying to sell you a loan. Keep the paperwork until the loan is paid off.

It is sometimes tempting to consolidate all of your debt into "one easy monthly payment." Be careful. Rarely can student loans be included, and furthermore, rarely are you going to really come out ahead in the deal. If you find yourself overwhelmed with credit card and loan debt, there are consumer help agencies that work out a payment plan to your creditors so that the creditors are happy and you can afford next week's groceries.

Remember that you can negotiate with credit card companies and banks these days for better interest rates. Considering how high your balance is going to become, it is a good idea to negotiate a decent rate at the beginning of the degree when the balance is still fairly low.

SUMMARY

Financial issues must be planned out carefully so that you don't find yourself beginning a program and then having to quit because you just can't keep yourself sufficiently solvent to continue. If you are one of those women who finds financial planning difficult to do, get some help from Consumer Credit or from a bank loan officer. The wrong time to deal with financial issues is after you've started classes, the bills are mounting, and the creditors are calling.

Keep your expenses to a minimum. Cars are a luxury in most urban settings and may not be necessary. You may not need to spend money on a computer right away. Do not buy a new wardrobe until you actually know what you are going to need in the way of clothing, and if money is an issue, go to consignment shops before hitting the malls.

Employment may be necessary. However, try to find work that is not going to compete with academics. If you work a full day in a demanding job and then take on a full academic load, you might burn out before you've completed your first year.

There are ways to find out who has the money and how you can get some. The Internet is a good place to start. Explore scholarships and fellowships before incurring the debt of loans. Use the fact that you are a woman to your advantage, and target groups that think of you as a minority worthy of sponsoring.

If you get loans, pay them back in full and on time. Others following you will need the money. Remember to donate to organizations that sponsored you after you graduate, and target their scholarship funds for women.

6

GETTING A
RUNNING START

In this chapter, we address how to get focused early in the program so that as the workload and the stresses begin to mount, you will have a structure in place that will make succeeding more likely.

STUDY SPACE AND OTHER NECESSITIES

Most women live in households with others, whether it is family by marriage or birth or roommates. If this describes you, you may not carve out sufficient space for yourself when you get ready to go back to school. It takes a great deal of space to become expert in an area, and graduate school is about becoming expert in an area.

In college, you got a little knowledge in a lot of areas and some focus in a couple of areas. Now, you will be developing focused and comprehensive knowledge in a couple of areas, and to do that, you will need space. The volume of papers and books you will have for each course and each project will quickly overrun a kitchen counter or a small typing table. We recommend ensuring that you have enough space so that papers, projects, and readings can be organized in meaningful and accessible ways. Even if you are very computer literate, it is difficult to get through school paper free. You will need a place to organize and lay out photocopied articles as you prepare papers. Often, you will be working on multiple papers and projects at a time, and they will begin to metastasize over every available surface in your home. Text and library books seem to multiply and need to be housed somewhere. If you think that the dining room table is going to be your study space, then make sure it is banquet sized. Plan to eat out most nights or eat on the living room floor because the surface of the table will effectively disappear by the end of the first semester.

This advice becomes even more relevant if you are planning to work and go to school simultaneously. You won't want to spend time reorganizing space every time you want to eat, study, or work on papers. Furthermore, the perpetual hunt for articles buried somewhere in that mess can gobble up time you can't afford to waste. It is possible to buy fairly inexpensive (virtually disposable) furniture that can be tucked into a usable corner as a way of organizing materials. You may not need a lot of space, but you do need space that you can organize efficiently.

It is also important that you have space that is specifically yours. If there are a number of you using one computer in the house, do not consider the computer table as your space. Things have a way of becoming a blended mosaic of ownership around a computer, and you can loose a great deal of time looking for something you know was on that table only to discover that it ended up in someone else's book bag.

Most discount office supply stores sell inexpensive stackable egg crates, folders with pockets, dividers, and file braces. If these are out of your price range, inexpensive file cabinets can easily be made from the cartons in which copier paper is packed. These are very sturdy boxes that are perfect in size. Most university support staff people will be happy to let you have them as long as you clear them out quickly. They stack nicely, have lids that keep papers from spilling out when you carry them from place to place, are letter paper sized in width, and some come with finger slots for easy transportation.

Make sure that you also have a comfortable and supportive chair. You will be spending a great deal of time reading, and almost everyone who tries reading in bed will find that more sleeping than reading occurs. Even if you started out alert, some scholarly works could successfully be marketed as sleep medication. Sitting upright gives you at least a chance of making it through a couple of chapters or an article or two before nodding off.

You also need to have a good reading light. Halogen lights can be cranked up so that they make an operating theater seem like a dimly lighted and cozy setting. Having your work area flooded with light not only reduces the chance of falling asleep moments after you settle down to read, but it also reduces eye strain.

Last, women under 25 can probably ignore this next paragraph because they have learned to study effectively in multimedia surroundings. In fact, they probably can't study if their sound system is off or the television breaks. Keep in mind that the reading that you are going to be tackling in graduate school requires full attention. It is often difficult and complex reading. Common household sounds can be distracting, especially in the first few weeks when you have yet to develop a comfort zone with the professional jargon and phrases that permeate the pages of the material you are reading. It is easy to become distracted by others wanting or needing attention, and the ambient sounds emanating from the rest of the household can make it difficult to stay focused. Get in the habit of closing your door and, if necessary, putting on "defensive background sounds." One of us uses a tape of the Pacific and Atlantic oceans crashing on shores to create a white-sound background. After a while, she doesn't really hear the tape, but she doesn't hear the television in the next room either. And if she does, she demands that the volume be lowered. Earplugs may be useful.

ORIENTATION AND EARLY SOCIALIZATION

It is tempting to skip orientation, particularly because orientation often occurs a week or two before classes begin. Most new students, especially mature students, are convinced that orientation has little to offer and will be a boring waste of time. We can't guarantee that it won't be boring, but it is a mistake to miss orientation. If you skip it, one thing you can be certain of is that each time you ask a question or seek clarification about a procedure, you will encounter someone saying, "That was covered at orientation." At least if you attended, you can come back with, "Not thoroughly enough, apparently."

It is generally understood that the catalog that exists when you register for the first time as an accepted student is the program you contracted with the school to deliver. The most recent catalog and an outline of requirements are usually passed out at orientation along with the latest listing of course offerings. It is imperative that you hold onto these until your degree is granted. If you are pursuing a profession with certifications attached, then you must hang on to these materials and all syllabi of the courses you took until you no longer need the documentation that you have met the profession's educational requirements. These documents may be needed when you begin applying for certification or licensure or a more advanced degree. It is conceivable that you will need the syllabi and the catalog until you retire from the profession because different states and different provinces have different regulations. If you move around, you could regret tossing out that "useless" catalog. Some women hang on to all of the course syllabi in case they ever have to document the content that was covered in any of their courses at a later date.

Most orientations provide an overview of the program. You will hear about sequencing of courses, prerequisites, minimum standards for performance, what happens if you drop below minimum grade point standards, whether you must receive a particular grade level in core courses to continue, regardless of your overall grade point average, and whether the program has a residency requirement (meaning full-time status for a certain number of consecutive semesters—not that you must live on campus, as one of us assumed).

You'll probably get a profile of your fellow students. If you are competitive, you'll have a sense of how hard you'll have to work to be first in your class. Even to a lesser degree, this does matter—if everyone graduated in the top 10% of their undergraduate program and scored high on the entrance examinations, you know that the grading standards are likely to be rigorous because student performance is likely to be high. However, if they admitted 80% of those that applied and the combined graduate examination scores in the class are substantially lower than your scores, you'll know that you may not have to sweat every test and paper unless you are one of those people driven to get nothing but A's.

Usually, there are discussions about program options, including part-time and full-time status and their interchangeability. Many who plan to be part-time students to try it out find that switching to full-time isn't a viable option and discover they are on the slow road regardless of their ability to handle the fast track. It is better to start in the fast track and move to the slow track, if you are worried about managing work and course loads, by withdrawing from courses offered in the next semester and thereafter paralleling the part-time program.

It is usually during orientation that students learn about how the department designates what courses can be used for free electives or advanced courses and which have degree-eligible credits. Furthermore, you will find out what courses must be completed before other courses can be taken and the degree of flexibility that exists in this area. This is the time to get clarification about interdisciplinary options and how many credits across disciplines (if any) you can take without having to exceed the total credit hours for graduation.

In addition, you will also find out what the restrictions are for interdisciplinary studies, including eligibility based on academic standing and prior-approval procedures. This is also the time to find out about joint degree options. Some schools and departments have interdisciplinary degree options available, and orientation is where you are likely to hear about these programs. And it is here that you are most likely to meet others who share your interests in combining these disciplines.

Meeting your fellow students and the faculty is one of the most important functions of orientation. A surprising number of women remain close to people they met at orientation, and some attest to friendships that have endured beyond the boring speeches and the revolting food (assuming they feed you). Many transcend the educational experience altogether and become lifelong friendships. As a personal example, one of us recalls meeting at orientation (in a "get acquainted" exercise) the person who was later the master of ceremonies at her wedding.

Remember that most people feel awkward and shy at these things. You don't know anyone, but most people there don't know anyone either. You are likely to find yourself making small talk about such mundane things as "so where are you from;" "where'd you get your undergraduate degree;" "what did you get an undergraduate degree in;" "where do you live;" and the ever popular "where did you park?" It doesn't matter what you talk about, it only matters that you start identifying fellow students you might want to get to know a little better. Many graduate assignments require that people work together on projects, and it is helpful to begin identifying early on women with whom you can work. In addition, if you are in a male-dominated field, this is an opportunity to develop a collaborative rather than a competitive relationship with other women in the program.

Meeting faculty members is another benefit of attending orientation. Frequently, new and established faculty people are there to get a look at you, too. Years ago, it was easier to spot faculty. They were the older white males. These days it is harder to figure out who is who, except that faculty members generally refuse to wear those "Hello! My Name Is—" tags. It is rare for deans, directors, and associate deans to miss orientation. It might well be the last time you see the dean or director until graduation, but you will be seeing a lot of the associate dean (some schools have multiple associate deans) and so this is a good opportunity to determine what kinds of things matter to those who are most in control of the program.

This is good time to meet the teaching faculty. You should try to get a sense of the gender balance in the department. If there is a very low percentage of women on faculty, they are all untenured, and they appear to be on the outskirts of the action, you may have a good sense of how the department values (or devalues) women. If all of the women faculty members there are introduced as being part-time or adjunct, you will have cause to suspect that the department isn't likely to consider women as full players or as essential to the department. This might be the time to think about where you might want to transfer to after the first semester. Refer back to Chapter 4 where we discuss the reasons that some women defer admission when they feel they might need a fallback school.

Another important function of orientation is that it may provide you with an opportunity to identify women on the faculty who might mentor you through the program. These relationships can be very powerful and can provide you with support as you move through the program. In fields where women are in the minority, these women can provide you with invaluable information about strategies that are effective in negotiating through the system.

Asking Questions

Yes, there are stupid questions in this forum. Questions about information covered before you arrived are stupid questions. Questions of a highly personal nature or are only likely to relate to your concerns are stupid questions. Asking questions on material just covered without seeking specific clarifications are stupid questions. Questions asked simply to hear yourself talking are stupid questions.

There are, however, a great many intelligent questions that someone should be asking. Pace the way you ask these questions against the information provided in the program overview. Make sure you get clarification about anything in course sequencing you don't understand. Find out what kinds of signatures you need to register for required and elective courses (some schools require advisers to sign off on registration and others don't) and determine who can sign if you can't coordinate with your adviser.

It is important to find out early what to do if you are closed out of a required course or if a course is filled in a time slot you need because of other nonnegotiable commitments. Different schools have very different ways of handling this, ranging from "too bad" to "forced registry." It isn't necessary to get into a detailed description of your individual circumstances. It is important to find out who can advise you about what to do if you have been closed out of a course because it reached capacity.

Determine what the guidelines are for adding, dropping, and resigning from courses and where the deadlines are posted. Find out what the procedures are to apply for leaves of absences and what the time frames are. It is important to know where to go to sign up for computer privileges, parking permits, student identification cards, and to get pointed in the direction of the bookstore. Whether you are disabled or not, students need to know how permanent and temporary disabilities are declared and how reasonable accommodation for them are handled on this campus. Remember, you just might break a leg on that ski trip you've planned for semester break, and arriving on campus in the snow with your leg in a cast is the wrong time to be getting this information.

Some students need to know how the university handles religious practices, including how religious holidays are accommodated by the school. Some schools may have no official policies, and so students may be advised to determine which faculty members are likely to adjust assignments or mandatory attendance to accommodate special needs. Ask for a schedule of secular and religious holidays that are observed and the timing of the academic breaks, then frame your question around those days.

Although we briefly discussed taking courses in other departments, you need to be clear about how your department will apply those credits. Some programs only treat them as "pass-fail;" others will assign the quality points based on the grade. Other programs are fully prepared to offer joint degrees. Get clarification about interdisciplinary course work at orientation if you really feel that you need to take courses in another discipline to develop the knowledge and skills that you need. If you're interested in cross or interdisciplinary areas, it is likely that others are as well. Get clarification about these departments and how many credits can be earned in another discipline. Some schools limit this option to students in good academic standing only, and others have a preset listing of interchangeable courses. This question can be expanded to include out-of-state and out-of-country internships as well. A number of schools, especially those in more rural locations, have arrangements with larger institutions for out-of-town internships. In addition, some institutions have "sister" schools in other countries, and it may be possible to do a semester in another country for full credit.

This is also a good time to determine who your adviser is, how long the person remains your adviser, and what the mechanism is for changing or keeping an adviser. Keep in mind what you want from an adviser. One of us never saw her adviser except for getting signatures and didn't consider that to be a problem. She wasn't looking for advice and used the adviser as a functionary. It wasn't because she disliked her, she just didn't need anything from her. However, others like to have a mentoring relationship with an adviser and would prefer having someone who is accessible and has an open-door, drop-in policy.

Once you meet with your adviser, you can get a sense whether he or she is knowledgeable about such things as course exemptions, appeal processes, and student grievances. You also might want to explore how creative they are about finding solutions to student problems. If you get an opportunity, you might comment, "Bet you've had some students with some pretty interesting problems," and see if they come up with an example.

The questions that every student in a program with an internship or practicum are burning to ask at orientation are how are they selected, how much input will students have in the selection-assignment process, and what happens if the placement is unsatisfactory. These are not stupid questions. They must be answered in ways that are clear to those attending. Find out if you need liability insurance if you are going to be in a direct human services internship. Make certain that it isn't just the school and the placement that are protected. If you aren't individually covered, then find out whether the professional organization covers student practicum liability. Listen to the answers given, and then ask additional clarifying questions until you are told what you need to know or someone suggests you should meet with them after the orientation for further clarity. Of course, you will be then considered the practicum expert in your cohort.

Different schools, programs, and courses have different attendance requirements. Find out if there is a general university policy concerning attendance. Each faculty person usually has their own rules about what they expect from students, so understand that the rules provided at orientation may not be implemented in all classes.

GETTING THE WORST OVER FIRST

A rarely-listened-to piece of advice is to get the toughest courses over as early as possible. You will be brain dead by the last semester, and that is not the time to take that "killer" course. If possible, make the load heavier at the front end when you are still excited about being in graduate school, not at the back end when you are trying to focus on finding employment. If you are taking a killer course, it is advisable to balance the workload, if possible, with a less demanding course load that semester because you are likely to have to spend a disproportionate amount of time studying and preparing for the killer class.

We will discuss this further later, but this is also a good time to find "study buddies" as a way of sharing some of the workload. One of us developed a study group for a statistics course where each one took a section, mastered it, and became responsible for teaching the others that content. Because it was a more congenial setting than the class in which to learn, we all felt we did better on the examinations than if we had struggled with the content alone.

COURSE SELECTIONS OR STABS IN THE DARK

It is frustrating to open a catalog and read over course descriptions to try to decide what courses and what sections of what courses to take with what professors when you've not yet met a single faculty member or fellow student. If you think back to your undergraduate course work, you should remember that good faculty choices tend to close out early. If there are multiple sections and one closes out first, make a note of that faculty person's name because it is probably someone you might want to sign up for at a later date.

Make an excuse to meet faculty members before you register, if possible. Usually, faculty folks start arriving a week or so before classes, so if you hang around the halls targeting faculty members assigned to courses you have to take or think you might want to take, it will give you a chance to see them before you sign up for a course with them. As one woman said, "It took me 2 seconds to realize that he was the scariest person I had ever met, and I absolutely never wanted to take a course with him." Don't spend a lot of time trying to get to know them. They are very busy competing for the copier, trying to get their syllabi updated, and preparing lectures. Pleasant as they might be, they may wish you would go away. Remember that you aren't meeting this person to have a social relationship. The object is to find out about them as teachers. Note if they make eye contact, if other students greet them as they walk by, or if students hang around their offices. The degree of enthusiasm for a subject is also important. The more enthusiastic they are, the more they will generate enthusiasm in their students. One of us had such an outstanding research teacher that she turned one of us from a math phobic to an active researcher. So, take note if he or she appears to be approachable (though busy), if the door is open whenever he or she is in the office, if he or she is willing to meet with you once the semester is underway, if he or she has more than one office hour posted per week, and if he or she has some place for you to sit down (even if you don't). These signs are indicative of someone who cares about students and someone who takes teaching seriously.

One of the best teachers one of us had would have rated positively in all of these categories. He was not, however, a dynamic teacher in the classroom. Students still flocked to his classes, even though he tended to drone, frequently lapsed into thoughtful silences, and occasionally got into tangents that were hard to follow. Still, his material was current and stimulating, he knew his subject, he thought about what we could learn in the 15 weeks of classes, he planned experiential activities that enabled us to put into practice the theory, and he cared deeply about his students' success. This is not a popularity or beauty contest. This is a serious learning experience that is going to cost you a bundle. So be an intelligent consumer and go for the best, not necessarily the easiest, teachers.

A number of schools now rate their faculty members using standardized forms that ask students how this teacher and course compares to others in a number of categories relative to other courses in the program—clarity of assignments, difficulty and volume of assignments, amount of readings, quality of text, teaching style, classroom environment, and usefulness of the course in the overall curriculum. Some schools post these in the library or in the school. Ask the support staff people where to find them. Important categories to screen for are these: Is the faculty member prepared, does she or he accept and encourage student opinions, how do the readings compare to other courses (usually a volume question), how clear are assignments (good teachers can be impossible when it comes to making clear what the assignment is and then downgrading if you guess incorrectly), and how much the course met expectations. If you can't meet faculty people and you haven't access to the course evaluations, there are a couple of other options you can use to select among unknowns. First is to go to the bookstore to note what texts the various teachers have selected for their courses. This is only useful if each section has separate texts or separate supplementary texts. In many programs, the main texts are the same for each section, but the supplemental texts can be selected by the individual faculty person. If the texts are in, you can skim over the books to determine if the books are readable. Whoever has the best selection of texts, at least in your mind, is more likely to share your view of the world (or at least, what is readable in this world).

Second, it is worth heading off to the library to do an on-line search of the faculty's publications to find out what she or he is writing about—with an eye to whether their interests stimulate you. Scanning faculty publications obviously can be exercised anywhere that there is a college-level library available. It is worth noting whether they are involved with research, whether they are controversial (this can be a positive), whether they seem to be evolving or are writing about the same things year after year, and whether they articulate a point of view with some elegance. It is, by the way, not necessary to take courses only from those who share your viewpoint. It can be very stimulating to engage in discussions with someone with a well-articulated alternative viewpoint.

As a caveat, that same dedicated teacher described earlier was a very dull writer. He seemed to have an instinct for the most pedestrian way of expressing himself, and his publications reflected his plodding way of approaching the content. However, that method was also what made him a gifted teacher for the tough courses. He brought the same careful and thoughtful attention to each learning unit, and he made sure that every student in his class had mastery of each unit before moving on to the next. Although some of us occasionally got bored with the pace, all of us tended to stand out in the later courses because our foundation knowledge was so solid.

Frankly, our colleagues may not share this next opinion. We are concerned about faculty members who assign only their own publications. As important as those sales are to boost the revenue over publication costs on textbooks, it would be more balanced if they also included other readings and other perspectives. Granted, some faculty have written *the* seminal or definitive texts, and it would be foolish for them not to use their work. Few texts, however, reach this lofty status, so beware of academic narcissism. You may find that these same faculty people are reluctant to entertain divergent views in their classes as well.

Some schools will make it possible to get syllabi from previous years. Try to get a few years' worth for the same course to see if there are any differences. Faculty members who don't update their syllabi tend to teach the same course year after year. As their material gets stale, so does the quality of their teaching. In addition, scanning a syllabus is a way to decide how structured the faculty person sees the learning process to be. If each class session is laid out, readings are listed by week, and the assignments are spelled out in detail, you are likely to find that the person teaches in a structured and predictable manner. If, on the other hand, the syllabus has only some sketchy objectives and an outdated bibliography, you may find that the learning process may be very unstructured, the materials dated, or the faculty person doesn't see their syllabus as a learning contract. These are, of course, gross generalizations. A truly gifted teacher may use the course syllabus as a basic target and then tailor each course to the needs and goals of the students in that class. These people are constantly reinventing their classes from semester to semester, though you might not know it from their syllabi.

All of this presumes that you will have either course or section options. In some programs, you are offered little or no choices in the first semester (which may be a relief). In that case, all of these suggestions become irrelevant—at least until later semesters.

REGISTERING

Pay close attention. This might be the most important information in this chapter. The earlier you register, the greater your flexibility and the wider your selection. All your careful course selection and scheduling can be trashed when you are closed out of a section or class because you didn't register in time. One closed section or course can create a shambles of your employment and class schedule. Remember, if it seems like a good course or time of day for a course to you, it probably seems that way to countless others as well.

As closely as possible, try to plot everything on your schedule for the full semester, using a calendar. Block in work schedule or day care first (depending on which is the most rigid). Next, put in religious observances and "must attend" occasions. If you know when your kid's critical activities are, schedule those in next. Then check out the courses and sections, making sure that all prerequisite courses are plugged into the schedule first at times when there is the minimal overlap with work and maximum overlap with day care. Read the course descriptions carefully to make sure you don't try to register for courses with prerequisites you don't yet have or for courses designated as advanced courses. It may take you a couple of shots to get a schedule that gets close to meeting both your academic and personal needs. Then, register immediately. If you don't register early, you may get your worst nightmare of clashing classes and individual needs.

In recent years, more schools have developed telephone and on-line registration. If you still are clinging to that old rotary-dial telephone or don't yet have on-line computer services, you'll be among those searching for hours for parking, looking for the ever elusive registrar's office, standing in line behind the idiot unloading a briefcase full of papers onto the counter while asking a million questions (which your 3-year-old could figure out), and experiencing a memorable encounter with a strained and irritable clerk.

If you register by telephone or on-line, you will have to settle for the comfort of home while registering without any hassles other than getting a line and determining what number to punch next on your telephone or keyboard. Some schools haven't gotten on-line registration up and running yet but do allow faxing in registration materials. This can be done anywhere there is a public fax machine available. The problem with faxing, however, is that you don't know exactly when someone will punch you into the system. Registering in person, on-line, or by telephone provides immediate information about whether there are still openings in the classes you are trying to access and whether there are other sections with openings if you are closed out of a course. Make sure that you have your calendar and catalog with you when you start the process, just in case you have to adjust the schedule or select alternative sections.

If you have to register in person, plan to make at least a half day of it. If the school is primarily using in-person registration procedures, it is an indication that they have a fairly arcane computer system. Try not to be impatient. It is going to take as long as it takes and the best defense is fairly decent reading materials and a sense of humor.

Recognize that if the school is using in-person registration, the first obstacle is going to be finding a parking space on registration day.

Consider the hunt for a space as an omen of things to come. Get to campus 2 hours before registration starts if it is first-come, first-registered, and you are locked into the schedule you have planned. Bring a book, bring food, skip liquids (for the obvious reasons), and make yourself comfortable. Some veterans of the long lines bring a small folding chair and their laptop to pass the time. Some use it as an opportunity to meet others in the program. Try to identify those who are a year ahead of you in the program, and pump them for information about faculty and courses or anything else you or they think is important. They are likely to be as bored as you are and will consider it a pleasant distraction. They can be sources of excellent information, and this is the time to apply that old social adage that most people like to talk about themselves and their experiences. It was certainly the way we screened courses and faculty.

COURSE LOADS—THE MAGIC FORMULA

There is no magic formula for course loads each term, though programs usually have maximum and minimum credit hour requirements. The best credit load will always be idiosyncratic to the individual student and program. Departments vary tremendously within universities, and faculty members vary widely within departments. Some faculty people dish out a steady load of small assignments, whereas others tend to focus on one or two major assignments each term. Some students find that courses by examination are easy because they have well-honed skills in recall, whereas others find terms dominated by examinations as a variant of nightmare or killer semesters. So any discussion about workloads must be considered within the context of the program and your learning (and regurgitation) style. Try to ascertain what the assignments and examinations for the term are going to be like before you decide on how many courses you can reasonably take.

Graduate reading assignments are very likely to differ from your undergraduate experience. The first thing you are going to notice is that the readings for each class are double what you experienced as an undergraduate student. Reading assignments may well exceed 150 pages of difficult and complex material per class session. If you are taking three or four classes, the readings are going to take you a great deal of time to complete. We will discuss some tricks on how to get through this reading more efficiently in the next chapter. For the purposes of this discussion, you need to decide what your reading comprehension and retention skills are in determining what your maximum workload is. If you are a slow and methodical reader, without skills in skimming articles for the salient content, then you might look at part-time rather than full-time programs. If you are also looking at having to work full-time or part-time while you go to school, then understand that unless you have a job that allows you to read, you may be struggling to be prepared for classes. Until you develop a pace, schools discourage students from taking overloads, especially during the first term. It is not uncommon to have students get to the midpoint of the semester and realize that they have grossly underestimated the time that is needed to complete the assignments. Some faculty people will allow you to take incompletes, others will penalize you for the incomplete, and some will fail students for not getting work in on time.

The key to managing the workload is to assume that you have at least 2 hours of readings and 3 hours of written assignments for every hour of class. This is, to some degree, a worst-case scenario, but it is better to overestimate rather than underestimate the time you need for class preparation. Do not assume that the first term is indicative of the actual pace throughout the program. In some cases, faculty members believe in easing students into graduate education, and you can get a false sense of the demands.

PICKING CONCENTRATIONS

Some schools require you to select a concentration early, whereas others allow you a year or so to make the decision because the first semester or year's courses are fairly generic. However, at some point, you are going to have to make a choice. It is a difficult decision to make in the absence of substantive knowledge about the current strengths of a program or concentration (as opposed to the purported or historical) if you are choosing during the first weeks of school. As faculty members leave and are replaced, the intensity and focus can change. You can make some erroneous assumptions concerning an area of study based on the name and catalog description. However, concentrations can have an impact on where you get hired, so do not be too casual about what you chose. Making the decision about an area of concentration should be guided by the following concerns: What are the required courses; who teaches in that area; are internships or fellowships going to be affected by the concentration you've selected; and will the concentration result in greater employability?

It is advisable to screen the required course workload for each concentration. Look over the catalog and determine if they have a "model program" listed. Determine if there is any crossover between concentrations and if so, how that is done. Look at the overall objectives for the concentration, and decide which one is more compatible with your goals.

Check postgraduation employment rates to determine what concentrations have the highest rates of employment in the current market and what ones pay the best salaries. Look at the classifieds over a 2-month to 3-month period to see what jobs are out there (you can use the library's newspaper morgue to do this) and what the requirements are for the positions. Talk to major employers (personnel office interviewers can be a good source) to determine what specific knowledge they are screening for at this time and what they think they'll be looking for at the time you expect to graduate. Then, tailor the concentrations and electives to cover at least the more basic content in those areas.

Determine whether the program makes provisions for combined concentrations and whether they appeal to you. Be careful to avoid doubling your workload. Some programs will allow you to take dual concentrations, but you will have to meet the requirements for each degree or area of specialty. You may find yourself with courses that can be used for only one focus area—not both.

Last, if you have some flexibility about concentrations, it is advisable to select an area that you should be conversant and knowledgeable about to be taken seriously in your field, even if it is an area about which you lack passion. This sounds like a contradiction to our advice about setting goals and then finding a program and an area of study to match those goals. It isn't so much a contradiction as it is a way of helping you expand those goals to optimize your learning and postgraduation employability.

Selina discovered that in addition to the areas she thought she wanted to study, the program she selected enabled her to take business-related courses. This was an area she has never thought about, but she realized that she knew almost nothing about calculating production costs. Because she wanted to move into digital-arts production after graduation, developing a good understanding of the production costs would be a valuable tool and one she could use to market her artistic skills.

It is important to think through how a particular concentration might compliment a weakness. Most people continue to read and study in areas in which they have an interest. Graduate school is an opportunity to develop some mastery in areas you might not otherwise take the time to learn on your own but might find very helpful as a means of marketing yourself when you graduate. The idea is to find a complement and decide if you should major in that area and get a subspecialty in the area of your passion or subspecialize in your area of weakness. Ideally, this should also reflect some market trends in getting hired.

SUMMARY

It is important to develop a commitment to the program as early as possible. This means setting up space for yourself, attending orientation, and begin thinking about the program of study you have embarked on in very concrete terms. Faculty members are the key to much of your learning. Find out who teaches what and how good they are. Figure out what the various concentrations are about in terms of course work and faculty personnel. Last, try to get courses that are likely to be the most difficult out of the way by taking them as early as possible. Meet your adviser and determine what he or she expects of advisees.

7

LEARNING YOUR WAY AROUND

In this chapter, we spend some time addressing how you can self-orient into the environment effectively and efficiently. Learning where things are early in the program saves time later when you, frankly, won't have time to deal with finding resources. We talk about strategies to save you money and time so that you can become a more effective student quickly, including new-student activities worth attending. Last, we introduce ways of clarifying with faculty the kinds of workloads their courses have based on information in the syllabi.

GETTING THERE FROM HERE

During the first week, there is usually a period of gearing up that gives you some time to explore the academic environment. The only way to handle the confusion of the first week is to treat it as a great adventure. This is the time to explore the campus and get familiar with the location of places and things you will need while you are on campus. This includes locations of vending machines, the box office where you can buy student-rate tickets, and safe places to exercise. So, how do you get there from here?

The only successful and sane way to learn your way around a large campus is to put on a good pair of walking shoes and get started. Understand that campus maps were designed and printed by demented sadists. They are rarely printed in type that you can read without a magnifying glass. They have buildings listed by names that you cannot find anywhere on the building itself, and you later discover everyone calls it "the complex," not the "Smathers-Reynolds" building. It is worth finding out what departments are housed in what buildings as a point of reference.

The easiest way to get started is to find a centralized landmark that you can find pretty much from anywhere on campus, and consider it the center of a clock. It might be where your department is located, a strangely shaped building, the most accessible parking lot from the highway, or some feature of the campus that can be easily spotted. This is never the building or structure on the cover of the catalogue (it took one of us 2 years before we spotted the columns featured in all of the brochures). Use that point as "noon" and work your way through the four quadrants. Start with the neighborhood where the library is located because you will be spending a great deal of time there until you graduate. As you work your way through the campus, make mental notes about where the bathrooms are (or even more exciting—where the clean bathrooms are) and be sure to note which ones have tampon dispensers. Also look for student computers and where you can get a decent cup of coffee. In addition, you might try a few of the dining rooms and fast-food places or at least give them a sniff test, with the understanding that campus food never changes and is generally inedible.

If you haven't done much walking in the last few years, then proceed slowly at first, particularly if it is still hot. Figure out where the water fountains are and what buildings connect to what other buildings. This information is very useful in very hot and very cold weather. Once classes are fully underway, you won't have time to do this, but you'll wish you had when it is pouring or there is an ice storm.

Parking

Accept as a given that the moment you arrive on campus, you will begin complaining about parking. There will never be enough parking regardless of how new the campus is. The older and hillier campuses have almost no parking, and your complaints are going to join the chorus of complaints of current students, past graduates, and anyone else who has ever worked there. Parking struggles are, without exception, the one thing that unifies faculty and students. They both spend an inordinate amount of time grumbling about the situation while looking for spaces. They complain bitterly about the barbaric behavior regularly evidenced in the parking lot. It is frustrating; it is impossible; it is outrageous; and it isn't going to change. The parking permit they charge outrageous amounts for only adds to the frustration because the permit is nothing more than a license to hunt for a space. We have witnessed fights in the parking lots over spaces too small for either car competing for it. If you think it is bad at the beginning of the academic year, understand that as the weather deteriorates, parking lots become more hostile environments.

It is advisable to tour the parking lots to figure out how they are laid out so you are in the best position to zip around as someone is heading for a car or backing out. This means knowing which way the lanes run and where the dead-end lanes are located so you don't get trapped. Knowing the parking lots is nearly as important as knowing the buildings. If you can't get into a parking spot, you can't get to class. We are convinced that parking lots were designed by the same sadists that put together the campus maps.

The trick is to find out how early or late you have to be on campus to find parking. The peak hours are usually after 8 AM until 4 PM on most campuses. This means that the evening students are only a little more likely to find parking. Last, parking is best handled with a sense of humor. It isn't worth having a stroke over, and most people eventually find a space. Just remember that the more remote the lot, the better your chances are of finding a spot. That's why we suggest that you learn about the shuttles.

If possible, get a campus map and determine what the parking-lot-to-building hikes will look like for the schedule you have drafted. Although this won't strike you as particularly important in September, it becomes extremely important from December through February or March in the northern states. Keep in mind that campus shuttles are always pulling out just as you approach the stop, and drivers will sadistically ignore your screams as you pound on the back of the bus while being covered with soupy slush from spinning wheels.

Shuttles, Spines, and Tunnels

Use your first week on campus to map out your classes and decide where you can best park, either for getting to classes or leaving campus by taking advantage of the shuttles. Take rides on all of the campus shuttles to get familiar with the routes. It helps to know where they go and to learn what direction to take them, depending on where you are going. As the weather deteriorates, you will be dependent on the shuttles along with everyone else. Figure out where the stops are relative to the various parking lots. The most distant lot may prove to be the best lot in lousy weather because it has a good shelter and the shuttles run more frequently. It beats finding the last parking space in the closest lot only to face the equivalent of a three-block walk in a driving rain or in blizzard conditions.

Find out which shuttles drop you off closest to where most of your classes are likely to meet. Also determine where the best drop-off points are if you need to connect to city buses or to other shuttles. In general, riding the buses around campus is a good way to get a sense of how the campus is laid out, which streets are through streets, and where the best bus-to-building locations are.

Next, make a mental map of important stairwells and elevators on campus. Elevators have a tendency to be slow and to break down with regularity. If your department or class isn't more flights up than you can walk without passing out, get in the habit of walking. It is great exercise and might be the only exercise you'll get. If you don't like going up the stairs, then consider going down them. Think of it as a way to preserve your bone density. However, do find out from others if the stairwells are safe. In one urban school, there was a "colony" of homeless people living on the landings. Some of us got to know them well and we tended to "look after" them. Although most of them were nonthreatening, a few were irritable if disturbed "too early" in the morning (11:00 was barely tolerable).

Universities located in very cold, hot, or rainy climates tend to have underground tunnels and overhead spines connecting the buildings. Often, these are not laid out in ways that make much sense, and these passages often require that you take less than direct routes, but they can make getting from here to there more pleasant in foul weather. They rarely save any time, and they often are on multiple levels, so you have to learn where to go up or down a level to reconnect with them. The tunnels are the most frustrating because it is easy to get turned around in them, and so expect to get lost the first few time you use them. Fortunately, some schools have had the good sense to put color-coded bands on the walls to help people stay oriented in them. Otherwise, like everyone else, you'll just have to surface a few times until you learn your way around in them.

There are lots of short cuts on campus as well. If there aren't tunnels or spines, you can learn which buildings meet and which doors are locked. You can learn which buildings you can pass through either to catch an elevator as a way of avoiding a steep hill or as a means of keeping warm.

CLASSROOMS AND TRANSITIONS

Some people like to check out classrooms before classes actually start. They like to know where they are located on campus and also to get familiar with the environment. If you haven't been on campus in awhile, you'll be surprised how little classrooms have changed over the last 20 years. For the most part, you will find the same small and uncomfortable desks, only these days, some are made of molded plastic instead of splitting plywood. That just makes them a different kind of uncomfortable. The lighting is still only marginally effective. As a result, there are advantages to checking out the rooms and deciding where you can get the best views of the instructor, the chalkboard, the overhead, and the outside world or the hallways. Good views can prove to be quite handy if you find yourself needing a diversion from an excruciatingly dull instructor or very dull colleagues.

Visualizing yourself as a student will facilitate role transition for older and returning students. As you sit there for a few minutes, you will begin shifting out of your current adult roles endowed with autonomy and authority into a role characterized by a remarkable lack of power and control. If you do it before classes start, you should have less trouble with the transition once classes begin.

FINDING THE ESSENTIALS

The beginning of the semester is the best time to get familiar with the resources that are available on the campus, including key people in those environments. We address a few of those, including the library, the computing center, tutorial services, day care facilities, and the health center.

▓ Libraries

Getting to know the libraries on campus and the reference librarians is one of the best ways to ensure that you will succeed in graduate school. Do not think that you can get through graduate school with only occasional trips to the library to pull a couple of books like you probably did as an undergraduate. The best time to get generous amounts of help about how to use all of the library resources is at the beginning of the semester when most librarians are standing around looking for people to assist.

For the returning student, libraries have changed a great deal in the last 10 to 15 years. The first thing you will notice is that the card catalogs, reference guide books, journal abstracts, and periodical guides have been replaced with on-line systems. It is a far more effective way to search for information than the old system because it enables you to combine topics and narrow or broaden the scope of your searches, but someone needs to show you how to do it. Generally, you will need a student number to access the systems, so make sure you have registered before you begin.

Ask the staff at the reference desk if there is someone available to show you how to use the general reference area. This often includes dictionaries, encyclopedias, and reference manuals in addition to the on-line search services. These days, you can find the tables of contents of just-published journals before the abstracts have been entered in the on-line services. More and more journal articles are on-line, and it is inevitable that journals will be on-line in the future.

Often in larger universities, a reference librarian is assigned to each school and department so that you can have access to someone with expertise in your own field. If that's the case, this is a very valuable person to develop a good working relationship with early. They know how extensive the holdings are in your area, which libraries on the interlibrary loan consortium have additional resources, and how to access the major data sets that the university has on-line (e.g., census and Centers for Disease Control tracts). They will help you decide which topics for study are well-supported by the current holdings and which ones will require a great deal of planning because you will be reliant on interlibrary loan resources. If the reference librarian takes a special interest in you and your area of study, he or she may well continue searching for information about one topic long after you have moved on to new areas.

Some schools have holdings that are too large for one building, and so they have numerous smaller libraries on campus (e.g., graduate, science, undergraduate, and law are the most common divisions). Determining which library has which set of holdings is an important time saver. You will discover that a book housed in both the undergraduate and the graduate libraries is most likely on the shelf in the undergraduate library. In fields with interdisciplinary foci, the librarian can help you develop literature search skills to address the overlapping areas of knowledge. In addition, they often know which women students and faculty members share your area of interest and can help to link you with them. In building a support network, these are important connections.

Some libraries house their journal collections separately and in alpha order (bless them), others house them separately using the call number system (which requires looking them up on the on-line system for the call number), and a few intermingle books with bound journals (you will learn to hate this as much as the rest of us). Unbound copies of journals (the most recent) are always housed somewhere else, usually where they also have daily newspapers and popular magazines. Again, this is the kind of information that you get either in a library orientation or from a reference librarian.

Libraries have new-student orientations that you should attend. Each of the on-line search functions have their own peculiarities of syntax and methods for combining topics, and it is easier to learn it the right way first. At the risk of sounding redundant, you waste a great deal of time if you go with a trial-and-error method of learning how to use library resources.

Definitely find out where the bathrooms are located in the library. Find out where the copiers are and where you can purchase copy cards so you don't have to carry hundreds of dollars worth of quarters around with you. Different schools have different systems for making copies, some of which are more student friendly than others. While you are at it, find out where the newspaper morgues are and which papers they carry. If you want to become knowledgeable about the historical context of a phenomenon, newspapers are a good source. The microfilm collection of some schools includes many federal and state publications and can be extensive. You may need to print off of the microfilm, so determine which fiche readers have printers and which of those makes the cleanest copies.

If your campus supports a law library, you will need to make a separate trip to their collection. Law schools are mandated by their accrediting body to house their collection separately and have their own law librarian. In some schools, the staff is unfriendly if you are not a law student, whereas others are quite accommodating to students from other disciplines. Law libraries often have complicated ways of housing their books, and it is easier to get a tour than to try to figure it out yourself. They also have an extraordinary on-line service known as Lexus/Nexus that gives you rich information about laws and policies. You need a tutorial to use this system efficiently. These searches are very expensive, so get clarity about whether you will be charged to use the service as a nonlaw student. Law students usually get free access to the service, so begin thinking about barter arrangements you can make with a law student if you need access to Lexus/Nexus and will be charged for the service.

It is useful to browse the shelves of the library to see what exactly is in the collection in your focus area. This knowledge will save you time when you begin to develop topics for papers and projects. This is not to say that you should tailor your interests to what is in the library. If you are interested in an area not well-supported by the book or journal collection, you are going to have to factor in time to get things sent to you through interlibrary loans. This can sometimes add weeks to a project and increase the costs substantially.

Computing Center

Next, you need to find the computing center. If you can get there a few days before classes start, you can cut the time you have to wait to open accounts by hours. These days, most computing centers allow you to open your account on-line. As long as you are registered and in the system, it is often a matter of point and click. The problems start if you are not computer literate and pointing and clicking is just another foreign language to you. If that's the case, then you definitely need to get registered a few days early so that someone can show you how to get on-line.

Do not, however, get an account if you are in a field that really doesn't require you to use programs for graphics or statistical analysis or you have those on your own system. There is no point in getting one if your classes do not require that you have an account. However, if you want to do library searches by modem at home; if you want e-mail access to communicate with fellow students, friends, and family; or if you need to attend classes to become computer literate, then this is a good time to get an account and attend whatever trainings you can squeeze into your schedule. Remember, if you get an account and don't use it for months, it will go stale, and you will have to be signed on again at a later date. If you have a computer and are not going to be using the university system under any circumstances, check if there is a computing fee and if it can be waived. Remember that if you do this, you may not be able to register on-line, and you certainly won't be able to tap into the library services from home, so there are some drawbacks to not using the university computing services.

▓ Campus Safety

On larger campuses, especially those in urban areas, it might be worth finding out where the campus police are located. At the risk of sounding paranoid, campuses are hunting grounds for thieves and rapists, so don't be casual about knowing where the "blue phones" are that connect you to the campus cops. More mundane, they have jumper cables, will let you back into the building you left your purse in, and will escort you to your car if it is dark and you have a long way to go to get to where you parked.

▓ Recreational Facilities

This next piece of advice may fall on deaf ears of those who should be listening and will be unnecessary for those who already checked it out before they got on campus. There is an old saying on campuses that with each degree, you will gain weight, especially because it is so easy to find reasons not to get exercise while you are in school. For some of us, there is the added problem of being in locker rooms with buffed up young people. On the other hand, many people are convinced that there is a correlation between moderate and regular levels of exercise and higher levels of academic performance. The advantage of using the university facilities as a student is that you can get access to good recreational facilities at a better rate than you can generally get at the local gym, assuming that there is a gym near by and you can fit it into your already packed schedule. In addition, undergraduates majoring in sports often can be hired as personal trainers for far less than you'd be paying at a commercial gym. The only equipment that ever seems to be a problem is getting into the pool at a decent hour. Swim teams seem to like to train late in the afternoon, so the pool is generally available before 8:00 AM, at noon, and after 7:00 PM. Doable but hardly desirable for most of us.

▓ Health Care Facilities

Some university health care facilities are connected to major teaching hospitals. These centers can offer a wide range of services either free or for very reduced prices. There may be a university health care policy that you are required to carry to be covered. If you are unemployed or underemployed, this may be worth looking into as an alternative to a regular policy.

Keep in mind that graduate school can be stressful. The higher your stress, the less effective your immune system. Even if you've hardly experienced a cold in your lifetime, you could find yourself with a blazing case of bronchitis at some point and wish you had access to medical care.

In addition to physical health services, many campuses have mental health services available, providing a range of individual, family, and group treatments. Most of these services are covered under the student health insurance policy or may be available to students at a reduced fee.

OFF-SITE CAMPUSES

As universities begin to provide more programs off campus, there is a growing tendency for students to graduate from a program without ever stepping foot on the main campus. These campuses are particularly appealing to those who are attempting to get degrees at night or on weekends as part-time students.

An advantage of making at least one trip to the main campus is that it will give you an opportunity to meet the support staff, tour the library and determine what the holdings are for your discipline, meet the librarian assigned to your program, determine what computing resources are available off and on site, and meet the deans and associate deans connected to the program.

These programs tend to rely more heavily on adjunct faculty members, although some schools make it a regular part of their full-time faculty teaching assignments that they teach a course or two off site. The problem is that full-time faculty tend to live close to the main campus and so are less than enthusiastic about teaching off site. They often lose the equivalent of a full day between traveling and class time if the main campus is some distance away.

There is an even more current trend to use something called "distance learning." In this case, faculty are located at one site and are televised to students at another. Depending on how good and reliable the equipment is, how big the screen is, and how clear the signal is, this can be a tolerable or intolerable learning experience. For students in very remote areas of large states, this may be the best way to get a graduate education but at some costs. What you save in transportation costs you may lose in the richness of the learning experience.

SUMMARY

Getting familiar with the campus is the first step to successfully getting through graduate school. The first week is when you can get the most out of learning your way around the campus and getting familiar with the library. This is the time to determine which concentrations or subspecialties can be supported by the resources on the campus. In addition, this is the time to get familiar with the layout of the campus, the location of places to grab a cup of coffee or a quick bite to eat. The more familiar you are with the campus, the quicker you will develop a sense of connection with being there. In some ways, the students who have the hardest time doing this are those in the evening programs. Much of the campus is dark or closed off by the time they get there. Worse off are those students who take classes in a satellite campus, usually located in a converted industrial park or at a local high school.

Get familiar with the environment as quickly as possible, and develop relationships with appropriate librarians around campus. The amount of time you spend in the libraries should far exceed your undergraduate experience, so learn as much as you can about what's available and how to use the resources before you find yourself buried under work and waiting for access to a system.

8

SETTLING IN

The First Week—
or Do I Really Need a Lunch Box

This chapter identifies some strategies that you can employ during the first weeks that will help you succeed in graduate school. They include deciding on what "look" is expected, networking with other women, and assessing your relationships with your faculty.

The first week of classes is a very exciting time. Universities often go into a form of hibernation during the summer and then spring to life the week before classes begin. For incoming students, this is your first opportunity to see what you have gotten yourself into for the next few years. Your screening of schools and the application and acceptance processes will suddenly become a reality as you sit in your first classes.

LOOKING THE PART

Understand up front that there may be considerable pressure on you to conform to whatever is the standard for dress and language in the program you are attending. Environmental norming is a very powerful force that descends on us in middle school and endures for the rest of our lives. The culture of almost any organization (be it business or school) attempts to mold people in ways that define membership (who belongs and who doesn't). The farther you stray from the rest of the pack, the greater the pressure will be on you to conform.

There are obvious advantages to conforming and less obvious advantages to not conforming. Either way, it is helpful to look over the second-year students to get an idea of what the long-term pressure on you will be about clothing. If most people dress idiosyncratically, then there probably isn't much demand for conformity in appearance. You might find that on class days, everyone wears pretty much what they feel like wearing. On the other hand, if most folks are dressed in serious business attire, then you need to decide what you want to do about your own personal dress standard.

Some lack of conformity can help you stand out. If everyone is dressed in drab blacks and grays and you love bright colors but despise blacks, then why would you dress in ways that depress you? It will do nothing to promote learning and may force you to take a trip to the mental health clinic for antidepressants. If the program is fairly rigorous about "professional attire" and you don't want to annihilate your competitive edge by wearing jeans and sweats, then find a tolerable compromise. Of course, dressing very conservatively in a freewheeling and creative program can create similar levels of suspicion on the part of faculty and fellow students.

There are, however, limits. Clearly, if you are economically marginal, this is not the time to boost your credit card balance to "walk the walk and talk the talk." Rather, if you want to dress in a conforming way, browse your closet to figure out what you can wear that accommodates what you can afford with what's expected. Conformity, however, should only go so far. If you cannot and will not learn comfortably in stockings and heels (many of us can't), then observe how women in the second year, who clearly can't stand stockings either, dress. Otherwise, your best option is to do creative, innovative, and incredibly superb work, wear what you like, and ignore the pressure.

NAME CALLING

Faculty

Different faculty people expect different levels of formality from their students. One distinguished national program has a policy that dictates that everyone (including faculty) is addressed by the titles of "Mr." or "Ms.," regardless of their degrees or age. A more common variation of this formality is one in which faculty are addressed by their titles, whereas students (regardless of degree or age) are called by their first names. This variation clearly indicates a perceived class differential between students and faculty. Some schools are extremely informal and both faculty and students are called by their first names, regardless of degree or age. Most schools leave it to each member of their faculty to decide what you and he or she will be called. The problem is that you really don't know what form of address to use until you ask or until they advise you about their preferences. One sure hint about what a faculty wants to be called is how he or she calls you in the first class. The more formal they are about how they address students, the more formal they are likely to be about their own titles. At the risk of belaboring this point, ask your faculty members whether they use their title and then respect their wishes, regardless of how much it irks you that they expect to be addressed by title but feel free to call you by your first name.

It can be awkward if you continue to insist on using a faculty member's formal title if the rest of your classmates are using first names with each other and their faculty. One doctoral school colleague who refused to succumb to the informality became the basis of a fair number of inside jokes among her fellow graduate students. Even if you were raised in a formal household with rigid rules about showing respect, it can make you stand out in ways that are not necessarily advantageous to you. It creates a sense that you are rigid and nonadaptive. Worse, it can border on intolerance, especially for students from other cultures where displays of respect are fundamental to interpersonal behavior. If you can't adjust, then try avoiding the issue as much as possible by simply not using any form of address or take the trouble to explain to the faculty members and your colleagues your dilemma and ask for their indulgence in the matter.

What Do You Want To Be Called

You are fairly much limited to be being called by whatever the convention is in the institution you are attending, at least in terms of the general formality of address. However, if you intensely dislike being called "Barb" or "Babs" under any circumstances, then you are within your rights to make clear that you go by "Barbara," and feel free to correct people who call you the "wrong" name. Try to be as nonaggressive but assertive as you need to be. It's your name, and you have every right to be called by it. The same applies to mispronunciations of your given or family name. Keep on correcting people until they get it right.

It is assumed that no woman reading this book needs to be told that she has every right to also reject terms that are inappropriate—either sexual or infantilizing in nature. There is no question that terms of endearment ("Honey"), or diminutives ("the girls in this class") are not acceptable, and most universities are more than willing to support objections to this behavior. It is best to bring any to the attention of a woman on the faculty and find out what your channels are for filing a complaint if you are deeply offended. If there are no women in the department (raising real concern about how the department feels about having women in the program), then go to the office of student affairs or the equivalent, and register your complaint there.

SEXUAL HARASSMENT

Sexual harassment is a problem that is taken seriously by most universities. Generally, complaints against faculty members are investigated rigorously, and some universities now have sexual harassment workshops to try to ensure that faculty members understand the potential problems they can cause themselves by inappropriate behaviors.

Sexual harassment is not only a faculty-to-student problem. In recent years, more women are reporting sexual harassment by fellow students than by faculty members on most campuses. Beyond the issue of unwanted and unacceptable familiarity, being stalked physically and on the telephone are also on the rise. On many campuses, it is not uncommon for women to report to the computing center that they are being subjected to e-mail sexual harassment. They often attempt to stop the matter themselves by indicating they are not interested and requesting that the person stop contacting them, or refusing to respond, only to find themselves being threatened.

Universities usually are aggressive about stopping electronic harassment and will terminate or severely limit computer privileges if the person won't stop contacting you. Unfortunately, it is difficult to make it a police matter because it is difficult to prove beyond a reasonable doubt who, exactly, is sending the unwanted material. Campus police, nonetheless, have been known to intervene and talk to the person you think is doing it. They also take unwanted physical contact seriously and will escort you to your car if you feel you are at risk. Keep in mind that people who persist in harassing are potentially very dangerous. As unfair as it is, as in any situation of this sort, you need to consider whether you need to leave the community if you are at risk. As is obvious, universities operate within the law and just as in the "outside world," you may need to take legal actions to keep yourself safe. Remember, if behavior is illegal, it is illegal, regardless of where it occurs.

Many universities have a basic "don't" policy concerning student-faculty relationships. There may be legitimate concerns about the power differentials between students and faculty members and there may be questions about whether the relationship can truly be "consenting." Some universities limit the "don't" policy to students in the same department as the member of faculty because they believe that the power differential ceases when the faculty member does not have direct teaching responsibilities for the student. Frankly, these issues are too complex to be easily addressed in formulaic ways. There is no question that some faculty-student relationships mature into enduring and equitable unions. However, if you are not certain that it is a relationship you want, then you should not feel under pressure to continue in it. Furthermore, if the university has rules against such relationships, it may be putting both of you in jeopardy to continue in it until you have graduated.

You have every right to have your boundaries respected, whether it is in a student-faculty or student-student relationship. You also have every right not to be exploited or treated differently because of your gender. If you think there is a problem, then talk to a woman on faculty you trust or the next person in the academic chain of command until the problem is resolved to your satisfaction.

NETWORKING WITH OTHER WOMEN

If you didn't go to orientation, then during the first week of class, you finally get to meet other women in the program. This is a good time to begin networking with them. If you can think of your fellow women as a resource rather than as competition, there are many mutual benefits for all of you. Women in programs that are dominated by male faculty members and male colleagues complain that they have been encouraged to compete against each other rather than against the males in the program. This can be done by ensuring that you are always placed on opposing teams or academic work groups. In programs where women

Table 8.1   Information Exchange Work Sheet

Name _____ Address _____ Telephone _____

Class Schedule
    Mon _____ Tues _____ Wed _____ Thur _____ Fri _____
Internship schedule & location _____
    Mon _____ Tues _____ Wed _____ Thur _____ Fri _____
Willing to share rides? ___ Yes ___ No
    Which days (check): Mon __ Tue __ Wed __ Thur __ Fri __
    From where _____ to where _____
Willing to:
    Divide up assignments? Yes ___ No ___
    Library searches? Yes ___ No ___
    Be in study group? Yes ___ No ___
        Days (check): Mon __ Tue __ Wed __ Thur __ Fri __
    Share family care responsibilities? Yes ___ No ___
        Days (check): Mon __ Tue __ Wed __ Thur __ Fri __

and men are more equally represented, it is possible to be more selective about which women you form relationships with, but it is still advisable to avoid overtly competing with another woman if you can avoid it.

There are more advantages to building collaborative relationships with your female colleagues than there are in competing with each other. This applies especially to women who are going to school and working or still have major household responsibilities. It is worth getting to know the other women in the program, determine who lives near whom and who has small children, elderly parents, or others needing care. It is also worthwhile to determine early whether you have areas of common interest and possible intersects between needs and assets. It might be worth initiating an information exchange. An example of the salient issues is shown in Table 8.1.

NETWORKING AND SURVIVAL

Few people are good at everything. Those that struggle to be may not live long enough to enjoy their successes. If women spend a few minutes at the beginning of the academic year determining where their skills, needs, times, and abilities intersect, they may find tasks that can be divided up or shared. The more you all cooperate with each other, the better all of you will do.

▓ Library and Article Summaries

If there is one guaranteed area of redundancy, it is pulling and copying articles in the library. One of the best ways to save time and share the workload is for each one in the group to locate and copy sets of readings for the others. If you don't collaborate in this area, one third of you will be copying while a third is trying to locate the journals and the remaining third is complaining at the circulation desk that they never can locate any of the journals. The time it takes to make five copies of one article is a lot less than the time required to make copies of five separate articles. At the beginning of each course, divide up the readings by library and call numbers of journals, and as equitably as possible, by the number of pages to be copied and duplicated. Set a deadline for all of the copies to be exchanged.

One group of very successful women also included a brief summary of the salient points for each article in a course known for notoriously difficult examinations based on the readings. They reported that this served two purposes: It helped guide the reading of the articles and the summaries became study guides for the examinations.

▓ Tutoring and Exchanges

Another possible exchange between you and other women in the program is tutoring. Clearly, people charge for tutoring, but it isn't the only way to get reimbursed if finances are very tight. In exchange for tutoring statistics and research methodologies, one of us was fed throughout most of her master's degree by women who couldn't afford to pay with money. Among women, the barter system can create a balance between needs and assets. Beside being fed, some women exchange tutorial services or editing papers for women less gifted in grammar or spelling for babysitting or driving. One woman was thrilled to trade her abilities in a course for the use of a washing machine that didn't eat clothing; another provided access to a sewing machine; and still another had a garden that needed tending that was seen to by a woman who missed digging in dirt now that she had moved into an apartment building. The point is, if women begin to build relationships with each other early in the program, the possible barter exchanges become apparent fairly quickly.

▨ Study Groups

In some disciplines, the formation of study groups is needed to survive. There are some tricks to successful study groups that you need to know before beginning. They are generally more effective if they are limited in size. Four or five members should be the maximum. Each member is a full participant and must carry her own weight. They need to be structured. They should meet at regular times. Each session should have clearly assigned agendas. Beyond that, there are many effective variations.

One group, for example, had each member handle a week's worth of course material. All of the women in the course found the instructor nearly unbearable to listen to and so attended classes only when it was their turn to report back to the group. They duplicated carefully prepared notes from the lectures and reported on all of the readings (with summary notes). When possible, they found the connections in the material to earlier lectures. They listened for buzz words and biases on the part of the instructor so that they would know what he wanted regurgitated back to him on the examinations. They reported that the group did very well on his infamous killer examinations.

A critical advantage of study groups is that they have the potential to become support groups of sorts. These connections often allow women to develop sufficient connections with each other that they can complain about their disappointment and share their successes with others who understand. For women who are in highly competitive fields, it also allows them a safe opportunity to talk about their anxieties and frustration either with themselves or the program.

The study group can significantly diminish feelings of isolation. Whether you are a woman who has not been in school for a long time, are living alone, and are entering a new field or are a student moving into graduate school straight from college, the sense of connection is potentially very beneficial.

The most obvious benefit of study groups is that they tend to keep students on task in their courses. They must be prepared because few groups will long tolerate someone who expects the rest of the group to do their work. The goal of these groups is to ensure that there will be shared mastery of the topics through review of the materials and critique of assignments. When each member works, the group is a powerful tool for success. If, however, you find yourself in a study group that is doing more supporting and complaining than studying and critiquing, then you need to decide if that is a need you have or if you need to find another group.

An important component of any study or project group is that the members must be basically compatible. This has nothing to do with friendships and everything to do with working well together.

There are a few things that can cause problems in these groups. If you have two very strong members competing with each other for leadership of the group and no areas where they can compromise or balance each other, you are going to find that the group becomes contentious rather than productive. If you find yourself in a group with too many "parasitic" members, you are going to find yourself doing the work while your resentment level increases. Keep in mind, however, that if you are basically an "idea" person but not good at details, you may well be doing more of the up-front work and less of the "backend" work.

It is important to determine what the potential balances are in these groups before you go group hopping. A group filled with idea people often has a harder time getting tasks divided up and monitoring for effectiveness. Leadership should shift as the tasks shift in the group. What is essential is that the group share common goals and have enough leadership and organization to define how it wants to achieve those goals. Last, each member should work hard enough to help all the members achieve their goals.

Part of your job may be to help the group stay focused on work needed to succeed in presentations, examinations, or projects. One technique for getting the group back on task is to glance at your watch and say, "As fascinating as this is, I'm a little concerned about whether we are running out of time. Perhaps we could finish reviewing the notes and if we have time afterwards, we could resume this conversation over coffee."

SUMMARY

The first week brings with it heightened excitement. This is a time when you will be in the best position to find other women with whom to network and develop study groups. This is also when you will begin to understand what you have gotten into as a graduate student. As you become more comfortable with the environment, you will also come to understand the pressures to conform that will be exerted by faculty members and fellow students. How you adjust to these pressures should be consistent with who you are and how you view your world but should also recognize that graduate schools expect some socialization to occur.

9

THE SYLLABUS AS A
LEARNING CONTRACT

In this chapter, we offer some suggestions on how to use the syllabi in your courses as learning contracts, save money on the cost of certain texts, develop study patterns, read and organize material for papers, and get clarification from faculty about assignments and expectations. Last, we discuss how to change sections, add sections, and drop courses with the least amount of hassles.

Many of us hardly glanced at the syllabi passed out during our undergraduate years other than to look at the dates of the examinations, what the assignments were, and when they were due. A few of us looked at mandatory readings for classes (and even fewer did all of the assigned reading). It is likely that most of us did not look at the course objectives or overviews. Syllabi were considered nothing more than declarations of what we had to do to get an A. They were rarely viewed as the learning contract between students and faculty, which is what they are.

It may surprise you to know that faculty members spend an inordinate amount of time arguing over the objectives of most classes. At issue is whether they meet the standards established by the accrediting body for that profession, what students are expected to know at the end of each course, whether all sections should use the same texts and assignments, and whether the courses are at foundation or advanced levels.

▓ What to Look For in a Syllabus

Each syllabus should have a general overview about the course content and where it fits in the curriculum. The overview should indicate the level of the course (foundation or advanced knowledge), what prerequisites must be taken to be eligible for this course, and what its basic organizing principles are. Each syllabus should include learning objectives that are sufficiently detailed so that you will have a general idea about what you should know at the end of the course. Most have the assignments indicated (the deliverables) and how they contribute to the overall learning plan. Some will also have outcome statements that declare what you should, at minimum, be able to do or know at the end of the course. Most have a learning plan of some sort, either broken out weekly or by topic areas. Last, most of them have a comprehensive bibliography about the relevant literature that informs the knowledge base for the course.

Different schools have different syllabus formats and there are varying degrees of flexibility within schools and programs about whether all sections of the same course have the same syllabus. Some adopt a master syllabus with identical course description and objectives for each section but allow individual faculty people to tailor the course to reflect their own core or advanced knowledge, as long as the master objectives are covered. Other schools or programs have a lockstep approach to the syllabi and dictate what will happen in each session of the term so that the syllabi are fundamentally prescriptive.

▓ The Absent Syllabus

In the first class, the faculty member should go over the syllabus. At the risk of sounding rigid about the importance of the syllabus, no faculty person should be standing in front of a class without some idea of what he or she expects to cover during the term. The following excuses are among the most commonly heard for not having a syllabus prepared before the first class: "The copier is down again;" "I just got the course, and I'm not sure what I want to do with it yet;" "I looked at the one the department prepared and decided we could do something different (more creative, less boring) with this course;" "I figured we'd just work it out as we go along;" or "Because this is a new course we aren't certain we will keep in the curriculum, it wasn't worth the trouble to put one together this term." Regardless of how creative and flexible the faculty person sounds delivering these lines, there is no legitimate reason for a course to be given without a syllabus. Make certain that at some point *early* in the term you see a syllabus. It could be a problem later if you ever have to document content of the course. Furthermore, if a course turns out to be very unstructured, with almost no content, it becomes difficult to argue that the course is failing to provide what you contracted for it you never got a contract.

The "We Aren't Using It" Syllabus

A variation on the absent syllabus is the negating statement that the faculty member delivers as he or she is passing out a syllabus. They usually begin by acknowledging that this is the official syllabus, but he or she does not intend to teach the course with either the text listed or intends to dramatically change the content from what's in the syllabus. Often, this is done somewhat conspiratorially with students. The same problems exist with this approach as exist with the absent syllabus. In either case, you have no formal or firm commitment with the faculty member about what you can reasonably be expected to learn in this class.

Often, this isn't apparent until you've been in the course for a few weeks, and you begin to realize that what is happening in the course seems to have little or no connection with the syllabus that was handed out. It is only when you question the faculty member about the discrepancy that you realize that he or she never intended to teach the content in the objectives.

The Evaporating Syllabus

There are times that the initial review of the syllabus is indicative that there is an adequate learning contract based on the objectives and the teaching units elaborated in the syllabus. However, once the course gets underway, the actual course and the syllabus have little, if anything, in common.

Lonzena finds herself in a business ethics class with a new adjunct faculty member teaching the course. The course, which was supposed to provide her with a basic understanding of ethical business practices, deteriorates rapidly into inane classroom discussions because the instructor has assigned 30% of the grade points for "classroom participation." As a result, students compete during most of the class to outtalk each other rather than engaging in meaningful discussions. Worse, she finds that faculty members in other courses expect her to be familiar with the court decisions and practice principles that frame some of the legal issues and principles about which she has learned nothing. These areas are not being discussed because of the circus-like environment that is emerging in this course. She is afraid that if she doesn't attend class, she will automatically be marked down for nonparticipation, but she also feels that the class is a complete waste of her time.

Lonzena's experience is not uncommon. A course that appears to cover the major issues or topics in a focus area may deteriorate into a meaningless experience because the faculty member does not have mastery over the content, the teaching style may thoroughly compromise the content, or as in Lonzena's case, classroom dynamics may undermine the attainment of the expected knowledge or skills for the course. This is not the same as a faculty member who articulates a point of view that you do not support or who tends to focus on areas that are different than your major interest. It is important to determine whether the problem is the lack of content rather than the focus of the content. The first is a violation of the learning contract. The latter represents a difference of opinion about relevant material.

Resolving the Syllabus Problem

The place to start is with your adviser (unless, obviously, your adviser is teaching the course). You need to be able to explain clearly what the problem is.

Lonzena met with her adviser. She explained that the course was more than half over and none of the objectives had been covered. She explained that her performance in other courses was being adversely affected because the faculty members were expecting her to know about cases and precedent-setting legal decisions that had not been covered. She described a little about the atmosphere in the classroom.

The first question that her adviser asked her was whether she had spoken to the instructor. She admitted that she had decided not to speak to him any further because she feared retaliation from him for criticizing his handling of the course. She said that she did mention to him early in the semester that she was concerned that other faculty members seemed to expect her to be learning things in the course based on the syllabus. In response, he indicated that the students were not doing a very effective job in self-directed learning. He then indicated that he was very disappointed in the class and that all of the students were performing only marginally. As a result, some of her fellow students had criticized her for putting their grades in jeopardy.

Your faculty adviser should be able to help you resolve the problem. It is easier if the problem instructor is an adjunct rather than a full-time member of the faculty.

The Politics of Complaining

It is more powerful if all your fellow students talk to their advisers about the problem in the course. Colleagues, especially untenured faculty members, can be regrettably reluctant to challenge the performance of a fellow teacher, especially a senior faculty member. An alternative way to approach the problem is for a group of you to ask one of your other (better) instructors whether or not they could include some of the missing content into their courses. Admit that you know that they have really structured the course to be rich in content, but you are very concerned that you are going to be missing key material because of content deficits in the other course.

Try to stay away from personality assassinations, regardless of how angry you are. If you focus on content, the faculty member you approach can then talk to the problematic faculty person or administration about curriculum problems in the course. Let someone know there are problems so that, hopefully, the next cohort of students may not be subjected to the same inadequate course. Unfortunately, you may still end up with a marginal learning experience in a course that may not improve.

Other possible paths to resolve the problem are complaints to the graduate school student government or the academic peer review committee. As a last resort, you can take the complaint through the academic ranks. You need to remind yourself that you have every right to have the course delivered as promised in the syllabus.

If you cannot get the faculty member to provide a syllabus that reflects the course, then you need to meet with the faculty and determine when you are going to get a syllabus. If they indicate that they don't believe in syllabi (or some variation on that theme), then it is important that you address the issue with the department or the program's administrative personnel. Usually, this is the responsibility of the program director, and he or she is a good place to start.

The bottom line is that each course should have a syllabus that fundamentally reflects the learning that occurs in the course. If it doesn't, then you have every right to raise a stink.

BUYING TEXTS

The syllabus will tell you what textbooks have been assigned to the course and may give you some indication about how the assigned text fits into the learning contract. Let's admit it up front. Some courses you take because they are required and your interest in the material is not likely to outlast the final assignment. It is nearly axiomatic that you will spend the most for the textbooks for classes you least enjoy. You know that if you buy the text, they will either be relegated to the "never to be read again" top shelf of the bookcase or they will be sold back to the bookstore within minutes of the last class, for a substantial loss.

There are some efficient ways to save money on textbooks that are not likely to remain in your permanent library. The first thing to do is to determine if the instructor actually relies on the textbook. Wait until after the class begins to see if the faculty member considers the textbooks as a reference rather than a primary source of information. If you wait, you may find that you don't actually need the textbooks at all.

The one problem with this approach is that if you do wait and the text is the core of the assignments, you may also discover that the textbooks have sold out. Recognize that your grade may be affected as a result of not having the textbook and coming to class unprepared. The alternative is to buy the book and if it turns out it isn't necessary for success in the course and you don't want it in your permanent library, get it back to the bookstore unmarked within a week, and you might get a full refund. Most campus bookstores have a return policy for the first week or two of classes as students add and drop courses until they get what they want or can tolerate.

If the book is horrifically expensive and you can't afford to buy it (or it might be that you can afford the book, but you really don't need it and you know you don't want to hold on to it), locate others in the class who are willing to share textbooks. You can then collectively purchase a copy of each text and sell it back to the bookstore at the end of the term. Once you have figured out the shared purchase cost and the distributed resale cash, the textbook isn't all that expensive. It may turn out that you like the course despite your initial assumptions. Gloria, you'll remember, didn't know her passion for statistics until her first graduate course, and she purchased the text from her colleagues for the equivalent of what the bookstore would have given them on a resale purchase. This works best with supplemental texts rather than with required textbooks, unless the book-sharing group is very limited and very responsible.

If the required texts are purchased using this plan, then planning is key to success. If the instructor uses the readings from the text to generate classroom discussion, then arrangements must be made for each person to have access far enough in advance of the class to be prepared. If the members are part of a study group, then the readings from the text can be included as part of the study preparation and summary for each member. Otherwise, each member must make sure to follow the reading schedule for the textbooks.

It is not necessarily a good idea to make copies of the text for the other members, even if you have unlimited access to a copier, as this can constitute a violation of copyright law. Saving money is one thing; breaking the law is another.

SUMMARY

The syllabus is key to understanding what you can expect from the instructor and what the course is committed to teaching you. Without a syllabus, you do not have a learning contract, and you will have a difficult time holding the faculty member accountable. Furthermore, there should be some direct correlation between what is in the syllabus and what happens in the classroom. If there isn't, you have every right to complain.

Once you have a learning contract, then you are in a position to begin developing strategies to be successful in each course and in the program.

10

THE ROAD TO "A" WORK

In this chapter, we discuss some strategies to enhance your performance. It is important to recognize that these are intended to make your studying more efficient. There are no substitutes for doing the assigned work. You are still going to have to prepare for classes, study for examinations, write papers, and make presentations.

ATTENDING CLASSES

You must attend classes. In some cases, this is a pleasure. Many of us have had faculty members who come to class well prepared, teach the syllabus with creativity and energy, create a stimulating environment in which to learn, challenge students to stretch what they know and develop exciting new insights, and who help students advance in their knowledge and skills. Those classes are easy to get to regardless of the time of day they are scheduled.

Most of us are all too aware that some courses are boring, uninformative, stressful, and occasionally offensive. These courses seem to never end and each hour of class feels like the better part of a day. These are usually the ones that the faculty members will penalize you for failing to attend.

It is important to get to classes regardless of the skill of the faculty members. Despite what most of them say, they expect students to attend. Attending class will provide you some indication of what you need to do to get the grades you want. You'll get a sense of what the instructor thinks is important, whether they will tolerate creativity, whether they feel your job is to synthesize and develop new perspectives or regurgitate back information. Worse, if you don't attend and then perform poorly on the tests or papers, you are in a fairly indefensible position when you attempt to appeal the grade. The instructor will inform you that if you had attended class, you would have done better.

One group of women found themselves in a large lecture class where the faculty member expected attendance, which was documented by an attendance taker (that's the only thing his graduate assistant did). He then spent the 3 interminable hours reading from the textbooks, with occasional comments about the importance of certain passages. The women developed a rotational system where they all occasionally missed classes to preserve their mental health, but only one of them paid attention during the class. The rest of them used the time to read other materials, edit their papers for other classes, write letters, or anything that they could to prevent being lulled into sleep. At the end of the class, the note taker would make copies of her class notes and distribute them to the rest of the group.

In some programs, students are expected to call the faculty members and report that they will be absent. Be careful about the reasons you give. None of us likes to think that you consider your other classes more important than our class. Some faculty members are unsympathetic to reasons other than car trouble or medical emergencies.

On the other hand, many faculty members would prefer that you not come to class with a bad cold and infect everyone else. So be reasonable about why you are missing class, and don't miss too many.

CALENDARS

Most students who do very well in graduate school keep detailed calendars with due dates for each assignment or examination as soon as they know when things are due. They then begin to develop a flow chart of when they will complete library work, first drafts, and final revisions. They also plot out study blocks for examinations and study group meetings. The more organized you are about getting things done in a timely manner, the less problem you will have with midsemester and end-of-semester pressures.

STUDY PATTERNS

Learn your study patterns early and make sure that you carve out sufficient time for studying that matches those patterns. You cannot survive most graduate programs by "pulling all-nighters," or "throwing a paper together" the night before it's due. It is nearly certain that this strategy will fail, and you will spend the rest of your graduate program trying to recover from lousy first-term grades.

Different people have different cycles for when they do their best work. Some of us find making coffee before noon intellectually challenging, whereas others find their days have peaked by midmorning. In addition, some people read well in the morning but write better at night. Others prefer to work during large blocks of time and would rather focus for 5 or 6 hours straight than to fragment tasks into smaller units.

Most people tend to put off things that they don't like to do. Some students dislike papers but have little trouble memorizing and regurgitating. Others would rather write a dozen papers than take one examination. Unfortunately, there is a high probability you will get an unpleasant mix of both papers and examinations, regardless of your personal preference. Get systematic about how you go about preparing papers and learning material for tests. It is important that you prepare both the time and a study strategy that works for you.

READINGS

One of the most important skills you'll need to be successful as a graduate student is to learn how to read a great deal of material quickly and retain all of the salient information. Granted, most of us are convinced that we mastered the art of reading before we graduated from high school, but this is a different kind of reading, and it requires some newly developed skills to master.

The first thing you need to do is to determine what the function of the readings are for each class. Different faculty members have different expectations about the role of assigned readings. Some faculty members provide students with the sources for their lecture notes so that they don't have to waste time clarifying points as they expand on the material during lectures. These faculty members do not want to be interrupted by students asking questions about content covered in the readings. Others expect students to have read the material and to engage in discussions about the points raised in the readings as central to the learning process. They see their role as guiding students through the readings into more advanced knowledge about the topic. Usually, faculty members who use readings in this manner will use a good proportion of each class to engage in discussions about the various points elucidated in the articles or book chapters. They expect students to have read the material carefully before class and to be able to discuss the issues comprehensively.

In both scenarios, you need to develop a sense of where the assigned readings are fitting into each section (which is another one of the reasons that a comprehensive syllabus is so important) and tailor your attention to the readings so that they fit the demands of the class.

If the readings are important to each class session, it is imperative that you develop a routine to get the readings done before class. You need to devise a reliable method of getting the readings pulled from the libraries. Usually, students divide up the readings and make each student responsible for pulling and copying a set of readings for everyone else. It is far more efficient than each student trying to get to the same journals.

Next, look at the articles relative to the assigned readings from the textbooks, assuming that the textbook plays a central role in the course. Try to determine how each article fits into the information in the text and in the learning unit.

Most academic readings are organized in a manner normed by the profession. In the social sciences and sciences, for example, most articles have an abstract that provides a summary of the key points in approximately 100 to 250 words. They will guide you in deciding where the reading is most likely to fit in the assignments. After you've read the abstracts, jot a quick note on each article about what the basic focus is of the piece. Using articles on domestic violence as an example, you might indicate that the article "supports criminal charges in all cases when police are called." Another article may "discuss liabilities in criminal proceedings," whereas a third article "endorses mutual psychopathology between victims and perpetrators." All of these might fit into the topic headings found in the syllabus or appear to expand concepts suggested in it.

As the semester continues, it will become clear that each faculty member has his or her own strongly felt views on topics. Some are willing to tolerate alternative perspectives, whereas others become condescending (bordering on the inappropriate) when graduate students challenge their views. It is frustrating and galling to have to hide your intellect in an environment that is supposed to be fostering intellectual growth, but it can and does happen. If you choose to challenge these rigid and intellectually frozen members of the establishment, then do so based on a thorough reading of his or her perspective as well as the alternative views.

If the argument doesn't seem worth it, and many times it really isn't worth the hassles, then find an alternative way to survive the class. One of us got into sketching caricatures of a particularly obnoxious and arrogant instructor. It created the illusion of paying attention and caring during the class (I had to look at him often to get the quirks of his face drawn) while providing endless hours of entertainment for myself and the others in the class. He was so uninformed and erroneous in his information that there was no challenge (or perhaps too much of a challenge) in taking him on. Worse, he had a reputation for being vindictive, making it undesirable to get into an intellectual struggle with him. The caricatures were far more fun.

Once you get a sense of how the readings fit together, then decide where you can best make notes that will be useful. This should be something that you do in a fairly routine manner. For example, you can make marginal notations summarizing the issues in each of the topic headings, or attach a summary sheet, or keep notes on the readings in a notebook. It doesn't really much matter how you do it, just that you get a system that works for you so that you can easily retrieve the information during class discussions or when you get around to writing papers.

One of least effective ways is to underline or highlight. There is a tendency on the part of many people to highlight what they read. After awhile, more of the article is highlighted than not so that the highlighting or underlining ceases to provide easy access to meaningful information. Occasional highlights, especially material you are planning on quoting, is more effective.

Once you get familiar with a topic, you will be surprised at how redundant some of the information found in the review of the literature or overview will be. Instead of reading every word, develop skills in skimming the repetitive background material and deciphering instead what the particular focus of each article is. Very dated articles are sometimes included by way of background. If almost everyone you read cites the same article, pull it. These articles tend to give a historical sense of the development of a particular area. If everything the instructor assigns is more than 5 or 10 years old, however, then there is a problem with the course, and you might want to review the chapter on possible syllabus problems as you begin to decide how to go about complaining.

Most of us have content areas that we read effortlessly and retain easily. Consider these readings as intellectual dessert. After a quick sample, read the more difficult and unexciting readings first. End each reading session with those in the area you most enjoy. The more deadly dull the reading is, the more likely it will put you to sleep. Therefore, it is important to make sure that you have a well-lit, non-sleep-inducing place to tackle this reading.

Another effective way to keep focused as you read is to keep notes on the readings as you go. Whether you keep notes on the margin or in a notebook, switching back and forth from reading to writing reduces the potential for nodding off or getting distracted. This is particularly important in the first semesters when you are just getting familiar with the language of the field. Many of those publishing did not begin as English majors, and consequently, the writing can be obtuse until you get comfortable with the literary conventions and jargon that predominate in your chosen field.

Once again, study groups are an effective way of managing the readings. If the group is cohesive and all members contribute effectively, it is possible to get through the material with a minimum of torturous readings. Furthermore, the obligation to prepare your portion for the study session reinforces study patterns.

ASSIGNMENTS

The syllabus usually has information about the assignments. Often, this includes the percentage of the grade that each assignment accounts for and the due dates for those assignments. As faculty members, we can tell you that most students turn directly to the assignment section in the syllabus and then skim the rest of the syllabus.

Here are some points to consider when thinking about the assignments. Try to get a sense whether the assignments are intended to confirm that you are learning the material in the lesson plan, to enhance the general knowledge and skills presented in the course, or to allow you to develop your own expertise in a given area. All of these are valid functions for assignments.

When assignments are intended to demonstrate ongoing mastery, they tend to be somewhat regurgitative. It is important to make sure that you integrate the material from the readings and the class notes. Some faculty members are not looking for students to be particularly creative. In fact, you may well be downgraded if you don't frame the information in the way it was given. These faculty members are not looking for creativity and innovation. They perceive their role as ensuring that you have so-called mastery over the content. Then, there are faculty members that are looking for you to synthesize the material and to bring together the prominent points in a cohesive way. Before doing the first assignment, it is worth trying out both approaches in the class discussions and see how the faculty member responds. If they appear to reward the integration of content with praise, then that is also likely to be rewarded in the written assignments. If, however, you get shot down for missing the point, then you've been cued for what they are looking for in the assignment.

In some classes, you are going to be participating in an ongoing project for the faculty member. This is particularly true in fields engaged in scientific investigations. Faculty members provide students with the opportunity to participate in guided learning on a research project. Unfortunately, sometimes these "assignments" can border on student exploitation, although that might be common in your field. The success of the project may well reflect the grade you get. Faculty members are no different from others when it comes to blaming others for failures and accepting successes as their own. What is often key to success in these types of assignments is to determine how much autonomy the faculty member wants in students. Some faculty members are inclined to "monitor" every step and to want to hover over you. It is their right, and a power struggle is not likely to be beneficial to either of you. Other faculty members feel that this is an opportunity for you to begin struggling with your own project and expect to do little in the way of direct supervision. Frankly, it is their call. Your academic survival and grades are dependent on how well they think you have handled your part of the project.

Some faculty members develop assignments as they go along, based on what they feel will best achieve the objectives in the course. Although there is some merit to this approach, it can be difficult to pin down the number of assignments and the value of each assignment when this model is used. It would be helpful to try to get a general commitment from the faculty member about what the assignments are likely to be, how much lead time there will be for each assignment, and what the general topic areas will be. The more driven to get all A's you are, the more this will matter to you.

Particularly during the early semesters, you will probably have a lot of anxiety about the assignments. As much as you may want assignments clarified at the beginning of the semester, it can be difficult for faculty members to provide sufficient intelligible details until you've been exposed to some of the fundamentals of the course. Often, the details remain elusive until the course content catches up with the assignments. If the due date for the assignment is getting close and you still don't have a clue what is expected, ask specific questions about the assignment.

If you are going to be doing group papers or doing presentations, you should get details about the assignments early enough to be able to do some meaningful planning. In addition, it is critical that you know if the topics will be assigned or if you can select them. In some disciplines, you need to know how the presentation or research teams are assigned, whether a grade is given to the group or the individual, and whether time will be scheduled to work together on projects. You should also get some idea about the length, the expected format, and the general outline for papers and presentations. In addition, you might want to find out if you can bring in an outline or draft of the paper for the faculty member to review.

Group presentations and papers can be frustrating. It is not uncommon for each group to have at least one member who is a "tag along." This person contributes little and often fails to attend the work sessions. In addition, faculty members do not always provide time for groups to work on the project so that schedules have to be made to get people together. Some groups opt to let members work independently and then have each member either write or present separately. Unfortunately, the final product may fail to be as fully integrated as it should be, and as a result, the lack of polish may show up in the grade assigned. If you are driven to get A's, you (and the other driven members of your group) are going to have to assume the workload of the freeloader or you will have to learn to accept lower grades than you expected.

Some faculty members have the good sense to give you parameters about how long they expect papers and presentations to be. If none is indicated, try to get a sense of the length of each paper or presentation and what kind of supportive literature they expect. Students generally are told they will need "enough citations to support your position." This is one of those times when knowing someone a year ahead is helpful. Enough to support your position adequately can be somewhere between 10 and 50 citations, depending on the topic and the instructor. Find out whether all or some of the articles should be research based, whether books and articles are interchangeable in the count, and whether there are any other requirements for the supportive literature. It isn't a bad idea to determine if the faculty member has written in the area and to cite a few of her or his articles!

Get information about the citation format and use it. A very fine piece of work can be severely penalized if you are using the wrong style for citations and references. More about how to develop, organize, and execute papers will be addressed in the section titled "Writing Papers."

Some faculty members use a series of small assignments to ensure that students are keeping up with the reading, whereas others will have only one or two assignments accounting for the whole grade. Don't take small assignments casually. A number of missed or poor grades on these can seriously damage your overall grade. Find out if all of them count or if you will be graded on something like the 7 best out of 10. Find out when these smaller assignments are given out and if you are absent, how you go about making them up.

EXAMINATIONS

If the course is examination based, determine what content the examinations will cover. Some faculty members test comprehensively, and others test against the material covered since the previous examination. Find out if you are going to be tested only on the readings or on the readings and the class lectures. If lectures are included, find out whether you can tape the lectures in advance. Many faculty members do not like to be taped, so this is not always an option.

Examinations come in the same varieties that you experienced as an undergraduate. The difference is that the multiple-choice segments tend to be more difficult and the essay examinations are expected to reflect greater mastery of the material.

It is not possible to cram for most graduate-level examinations. They are likely to require that you know the material cold, and faculty members rarely grade on a curve. Some faculty members are notorious for asking the most obscure information that they can to weed out students.

There is no question that examination grades measure exam-taking skills. There are some things that you can do to help you develop better skills in taking tests. If you know that the questions are multiple choice, then develop flash cards. Most multiple-choice examinations test one's recall ability. Therefore, on one side, place key words and on the other side, place descriptors or facts related to the key concept. They can be pulled out while waiting for lectures to begin, while sitting in commuter traffic, or, for those of you fortunate enough to ride public transportation, while on the bus or train. Mix up the cards, and work both sides. That way, you learn to define key concepts, and you learn to identify key concepts from descriptor variables.

If the tests are likely to be essays, then spend a few study sessions learning to write out key issues. Look back over the notes, and make topic headings for the areas that the faculty member considers to be essential. Understand that the key to a good grade in an essay examination is to cram as much information as you can about a topic in a limited amount of time. The more you regurgitate and synthesize on each question, the more likely you are to do well. Keep in mind during the practice session that the favorite questions are the compare-and-contrast type. By now, of course, you don't need anyone to tell you that you must read the question carefully and confine your answers to the questions asked

WRITING PAPERS

Writing papers for graduate school is a very different exercise than the papers most people prepared in college. Beside complaining about the parking on campus, graduate faculty members constantly complain about how poor graduate papers are, especially during the first term or two until we have retrained the survivors. Unlike undergraduate instructors who may complain and then adjust their standards, few graduate faculty members will adjust standards. Some even seem to take sadistic pleasure in failing students. Therefore, learn from the early papers you write what is expected, with the knowledge that the farther along you go, more will be expected and less will be forgiven.

Organizing Readings

Good papers in graduate school are informed papers. Unless you have been asked for "reaction papers," faculty members are generally more interested in your ability to read, understand, and synthesize the relevant literature than reports of your own personal warm and fuzzy feelings about a topic.

You must spend time in the library to write graduate papers. If you don't have time to go to the library, you don't have time to do graduate work. It is that simple.

Furthermore, good students browse journals as they pull articles they located in on-line literature searches to see what else is available on the topic or on related topics. Many journals are now putting out topic-specific special issues, and you may find articles that somehow didn't show up on your search if you spend some time looking through the table of contents. As you pull books, you may find others that might help you formulate a question or integrate a complementary or contrasting perspective.

Getting to the library early is especially important if the topic is assigned. If you wait too long, you will find the shelves stripped a couple of weeks before the paper is due. If you do find something on the shelves, it is likely to be very out of date, on the fringe, or otherwise worthless.

If you get to select the topic (usually within a prescriptive range of areas), it is worth making a preliminary expedition to the library to determine what topics are going to have the most interesting and available material on them. If this is your first trip, it is also a good time to get to know the reference librarians, especially the one assigned to your area. They can give you a guided tour of the electronic search functions and the library's holdings on various topics, which can help you formulate a theme for the paper.

The importance of learning how to use the electronic search features of the on-line library systems has already been discussed. You can expand or narrow your search as much as needed to get relevant materials. Most of you should know that the title and the abstracts of articles often promise more than they deliver. You will probably discard half of what you pull as you begin to narrow the readings to support your topic.

As you browse the articles and books that you have pulled, scan the citations at the end. You will notice that there are a few citations that appear across most of the literature on that topic. You need to locate those articles or books because they are generally going to be fairly key to your understanding of the subject or they reflect the seminal writing on it. In addition, sometimes, you are lucky enough to find a meta-analysis (a statistical technique used to summarize large numbers of studies) of a given topic. These are treasures if they are good because they have often pulled together the current major studies in an area (and, as a result, have a comprehensive bibliography attached).

▧   Defining and Narrowing the Topic

Once you have decided on a topic, you are going to have to narrow it down into a focus area. If the topic is too global, it is difficult to organize the readings into meaningful categories, and the paper is likely to be too superficial or too scattered as you try to incorporate all of the information. For example, "child abuse" is a very broad topic encompassing many different types and possible causes. You would want to focus on a particular aspect of the problem (e.g., substance-use patterns in abusers), or the evolution of social concern about the problem (e.g., legislation and the media), or the political or legal aspects of the issue (e.g., the legislative changes in the last 5 years), or the current explanatory theories of causation (e.g., poverty and ne-glect), or the expansion of the concept into other areas (e.g., testimony and the legal rights of children vs. their abusers) before you had a manageable topic.

Depending on the subject you select, you may want to focus primarily on the research that has been done or the areas of contro-versy. The focus may be one that particularly interests you, or it can be shaped by what is available in the library. What is critical is that the paper must have an organizing topic area, and the literature that you use must demonstrate how well you know the area.

▧   Writing a Review of the Literature

Graduate papers either *begin* with a review of the literature or *are* fundamentally a review of the literature. Remember that the purpose of the review of literature is to examine and integrate relevant and salient literature into some kind of a coherent whole. It is not a series of book reports or article summaries. To do this effectively, you need to be organized about how you collect, read, and summarize the articles and books you pull from the library.

Searches take time, and good searches take a lot of time. You begin by using the on-line search features available at the library, scanning the bibliographies to determine which articles are repeatedly cited, pulling those articles to assess the current and past positions on the topic.

Once you have gotten the literature pulled, you need some way of systematically cataloging the information that you find. Most people develop their own system for making notes on what is read so that information can be retrieved when you write the paper. We will offer a few possible mechanisms, but you need to develop something that works for you. For example,

- Decide some broad organizational schemata for the paper (e.g., chronological, theoretical, variables, or research methodologies).

- Depending on where this article fits in the organizational schemata, make marginal notes about possible content fit in your paper: introduction, major theories or theoreticians, contributors-detractors to the position you are taking, originators or supporters of a theory, sequential question formulation over the history of the topic, summary section, or research methodology section.

- Use highlighters to discriminate items you may want to synthesize into the paper by using separate colors for each key section.

- To avoid using too many quotes, write summaries of the salient issues that you learn from the articles or books at the top, without looking at the actual language of the article.

- Look over the notes to determine the common threads and points of divergence so that you can synthesize into the major themes, issues, or conflicts that make a coherent whole.

At this point, some women write up an outline to structure the paper based on the information they find in the literature. Others begin writing to get a feel for how the material best fits together. The outline is important if you haven't done much writing as an undergraduate because it helps eliminate redundancies. As you are reading, look for articles that you think do an especially nice job of organizing a similar topic. Make an outline of the paper to see how it was done, and then substitute your topics and subtopics for theirs.

One of the advantages of using summary notes in writing papers is that it will help you avoid writing papers that are either strings of quotations loosely joined with a few words or sentences or outright plagiarism. Papers too heavy on quotations are likely to be downgraded for a number of reasons. For one thing, most authors have very different writing styles, so the paper will not hang together very well. Furthermore, it is difficult to synthesize material from different perspectives if the paper is a series of stand-alone quotes. Remember, your job is to bring together published information about a topic in a way that informs the reader in a meaningful way.

Part of the function of doing a review of the literature is that it should help you become informed about differing points of view. Your ability to become an expert in the area is to be fully aware of these differing perspectives and to be able to discuss intelligently the points of controversy. If there are two very strong opposing perspectives, recognize the dissenting point of view and then support the point of view of the perspective you endorse.

Significance

You will want to address the significance of the problem or topic under discussion. In the sciences and social sciences, one often begins with the statement about why the topic or problem should be considered significant at this time. In addition, generally there is some indication about what populations are affected, how widespread the problem is believed to be, whether it is increasing or decreasing, and what the possible causative agents might be. Once the nature and the significance of the topic has been covered, often there is some mention about prior work in the area.

Prior Work in the Area

In this portion, explore what else has been done in the area or in related areas. For example, you may be interested in how women who were infected with HIV because their spouses used intravenous drugs feel about it. You may explore parallels in the victim role seen in domestic violence cases. You would search the literature in areas involving HIV transmission where the person is known. You might look at the domestic-violence literature that deals with abusive relationships. You would evaluate if most of the material is based on case reports (individual women reporting their feelings) or on some larger survey of women. It is important that this material be organized tightly. It is important that you make a decision about how the topic can be best organized. Some possible options include reviewing the chronology, the prominent variables, the research methodologies, or principal findings.

Headings

Use headings. If the instructor has provided a basic outline for the paper, then use it to organize the sections and provide the reader (and grader) with indications that you are covering the requested topics. Headings should be bolded or underlined so that they stand out. The headings should be expanded into subheadings to demonstrate how you are bringing together the material you've selected for your topic. As much as possible, keep the headings in some logical or supported order.

Grammar and Sentence Structure

Do not expect to get good grades for lousy writing. Back in the section on application essays, we mentioned that good writing is a given in graduate school, and poor writing is likely to be penalized severely.

Sentences are the first indication of your writing skills. They do not have to be long and convoluted. Few of us can sustain multiple compound complex sentences in a single paragraph and not leave the reader a bit breathless. Granted, William Faulkner made such sentences into an art form, but Ernest Hemingway also won the Noble Prize for writing eloquent, simple sentences. Long and twisted sentences are not the sign of a competent writer, and they are likely to come across as unreadable.

Paragraphs are the next indication of the skill of a writer. Some students have turned in papers with sentences that ramble endlessly in paragraphs that never seem to end. Paragraphs should be about one general area of discussion. Look at the beginning and the end of the paragraph to make sure that they have at least a nodding acquaintance with each other. If the beginning and end are too radically different, you've probably got at least one or more paragraphs in there.

Plagiarism

Do not plagiarize. It is taken very seriously in many schools, and in some, a determination that a paper has been plagiarized may be grounds for immediate dismissal. Some faculty members, suspecting plagiarism, will spend many hours in libraries until they find the article or chapter you used (one of the authors of this book has been known to do just that).

Conclusions

For many of us, the hardest part to write is the conclusion. You've brilliantly pulled together all of this material, which you have summarized, integrated, and analyzed. Now, you have to tell the reader what it all means. It is tempting to resummarize what you've just said. Basically, this section should say something about the implications of what you have found. In essence, the conclusion should address a little of the implicit "so what?" Try to determine what the unanswered questions are and how they might be addressed. Deal with what might happen if the current trend continues. Most important, try to keep the conclusion consistent with how you've organized the paper. If you are looking at the evolution of the issue, then speculate where the current trends might lead. If you have looked at variables, then address the unexplored but possibly equally contributory variables.

Generally, graduate papers do not contain original thinking. The originality is in how you organize and present the materials you have read in the literature. It is a way for you to demonstrate to your profession your growing expertise in an area of knowledge.

As a caveat, if you are going to diverge radically from the assigned topic, then clear it with the professor before you start. One of us had a student who wanted to synthesize a theory from physics with a social theory. The student was advised that a faculty member from the department of physics would be asked to review the accuracy of that material and that half of the grade would reflect how well that material was presented. The selection of quirky topics, or topics in which a fundamental belief system is imposed on a basically unrelated field of study, can get you into trouble unless you are an extremely gifted thinker and writer.

SUMMARY

Getting top grades is a matter of planning and persistence. Whereas innate intelligence got you into the program, getting out is going to take a great deal of effort on your part.

If you read what it takes to do well academically, you understand why we have recommended essentially mindless part-time work. Libraries are going to become your second home. Unless you are in a program that mandates that you watch television, you will find yourself out of the television mainstream. New shows will come and go, and you will have no idea what your kids and friends are talking about most of the time. If you are lucky, you will have an opportunity to glance at the headlines on a semidaily basis to reassure yourself that there is a world outside of school and home.

Most successful graduate papers and projects take a great deal of work, even for mediocre grades. They may require multiple writings and rewritings to be graded as B work and a great deal of work to be considered A work. Although grade inflation exists in graduate school, it is less prevalent than in undergraduate programs.

Develop work patterns early that allow you to get everything done well and on time. Figure out a way to manage the courses you hate well enough that they do not drag down your overall grade point average. Develop some ability to self-analyze your best study patterns, and carve out the time you need to get it all done. This is why we also suggested that you might want to get an agreement in writing from your family about all the help they were going to give you to make this possible. In the long run, it is easier to make A's than it is to try to clean up a bad start in the program.

11

SWIMMING RATHER
THAN SINKING

At some point, you may decide that you are in over your head. This may be because you failed to adjust your study patterns to the demands of graduate school or because unanticipated emergencies created havoc out of your otherwise well-organized schedule. If this happens, you have a few options you might want to consider before dropping out of the program, depending how far along in the semester you are.

NEGOTIATING DEADLINES

If it is early enough, it may be possible to negotiate deadlines for deliverables with or without penalties. Each faculty member handles it differently. Some will allow you to set a new deadline with them as long as it isn't done the day the paper is due. Others indicate that the decision is yours, but they will treat the paper as late and mark it down accordingly. Others are very rigid about deadlines and will fail you if you are late. It is best to approach each faculty member separately and determine what papers or projects can be shifted and what cannot.

Although it is probably self evident, examinations usually have the least flexible deadlines. Most faculty members struggle to do one examination and are not very pleasant about the possibility of doing two, one especially for you. Group projects are essentially in the same category. In shifting your deadline, your colleagues have to shift theirs as well, and that may screw up their schedules. So anticipate that courses primarily graded by examinations and group projects will have less flexible deadlines.

Once you've figured out what faculty members are most likely to allow you to negotiate for a new deadline with the least penalty, then determine when you can get the work done and establish new deadlines. Do not miss the new dates agreed to by you and the faculty members. If you do, the faculty members may feel that their good will is being abused.

INCOMPLETES

You may decide that you are not going to get everything done by the end of the semester, even with extended deadlines. Incompletes are a way to negotiate with faculty members about when the work can be completed after the semester is over. Be careful about taking too many incompletes. In many schools, they convert to F's after a semester, so find out exactly what the policy is in your university. If you want to keep your grades intact, be sure that you are clear about what the penalties are for taking incompletes. Beside the potential conversion to a failing grade, in many programs you may not proceed into the next course without completing all of the prerequisite course work. It is possible that one incomplete could put you out of the program for a year or more until your course work is current.

It is probably advisable to develop a written contract with each faculty member about what you have agreed to before you leave the office. This includes the new dates assignments are due and any changes in the deliverables from what was initially on the syllabus or the assignment handout. It is also imperative that you keep the number of incompletes to a minimum. They are very seductive. Once you get one, you begin to think of the course as completed, although it is not. After awhile, maintaining a high enough level of interest in the topic to complete the work gets harder and harder.

Incompletes have another potential problem. If you develop a reputation as a student who takes a lot of incompletes, then faculty members begin to take you less seriously as a scholar. This can affect your internship placement, what fellowships or assistantships you get, and it can certainly have an effect on whether or not you qualify for scholarships and loans. So as a final warning: Do not take any more incompletes than you absolutely have to, and then, get the work done as quickly as possible once you've taken one.

DROPPING COURSES

Another possible option is to withdraw from a course. In most universities, there are deadlines for withdrawing with minimal penalties. Usually, as the semester continues, you get less and less money back when you withdraw. In addition, usually after the midpoint in the semester, many schools allow the faculty member to indicate what your academic standing was at the point you withdrew. Your transcript may well show that you withdrew from a course with a failing grade. Although this doesn't affect your overall grade point average, it can be seen as a possible blot on your record.

Withdrawing from a class makes sense if you think you have taken too many courses and cannot effectively juggle work, home, and school responsibilities. Additional reasons include finding yourself closed out of a section and defaulting into a section with a faculty member who may have little mastery over the course content—content you believe is critical to your success in the field. Other reasons for withdrawing from a course can involve health problems, economic problems, or concerns about your mastery of foundation course work that is somehow compromising your ability to gain mastery over a current course. Usually, your adviser will want some explanation about why you are dropping a course. It is not uncommon for students to take a course at an undergraduate level (which will not count toward your total graduate credits) to ensure that they have sufficient competency to handle the advanced course content.

If you remember, we suggested that you should begin in the full-time program and then go into the part-time program if you become concerned about successfully competing in the fast lane. Which course you drop, if you plan to switch into a part-time program, is critical. It is not necessarily the course you are having the most trouble with at the time you make the decision. You need to meet with your adviser and determine how the courses you are currently taking parallel the part-time program, and then, drop the course or courses that are offered next in the schedule. Remember that in some programs, you have to reapply as a part-time student, so you may need to make a good case for why you are switching programs.

TUTORS

Another common way to avoid sinking is to get a tutor. If possible, talk to your adviser or to someone who knows the students ahead of you, and get a fellow student to tutor you. Tutors from the same degree program have the advantage of knowing exactly what is expected and helping you develop knowledge and skills that are specific to succeeding in this program. If possible, avoid the generic tutors that put up advertising fliers all over campus. They are less likely to help you develop program-specific understanding of the issues and concerns, and they rarely are versed in the jargon that dominates some fields.

If you are aware that there are a few of you having the same trouble, determine if the tutor would be willing to provide you with a group rate. It can be far more cost effective for all of you if you meet on campus 1 day a week than if each of you tries to schedule separate appointments with a tutor. This can be an extension of your study group. If you all blew an examination badly, rather than necessarily disbanding, it might be worth getting a tutor for the group. If you work together well and basically get along, the problem may be that none of you are sufficiently grounded in one area, and a tutor may help your group master some basic knowledge that makes the rest of the content fall into place.

Tutors may have set fees. However, in some women's groups, tutoring often uses basic bartering. One group had women with a variety of skills and needs that were complementary. Bartered payment included transportation, sewing, cooking (a student from China taught the rest how to cook various Chinese dishes in exchange for both tutoring and proofreading of her papers), family care (child and elder care), and gardening (one woman going through garden withdrawal in a city apartment exchanged tutoring in statistics for an opportunity to put in a vegetable garden).

USING YOUR ADVISER

Your adviser should be advised if you are in academic trouble as soon as you are aware that there is a problem. You definitely want your adviser as an ally. It also helps if you have at least a nodding acquaintance with her or him before the problem emerges.

Advisers are in a position to do some of the negotiating you will need. If you meet with her or him to lay out what courses are a problem and are honest about the sources of the problem, many will go out of their way to help you develop an effective corrective plan.

Good advisers know the resources available on campus and can expedite your getting access to them. They may be able to get you into writing labs if you are getting killed on papers. They may offer to look at drafts of your papers and help you understand why your papers are falling short of graduate expectations. Many advisers are aware of good tutors who can help you get back on track. For those of us lucky enough to have a good mentoring relationship with our adviser, we find that she or he can intercede with faculty members to negotiate deadline changes or alternative assignments.

If you have declared a disability, your adviser needs to be aware of what kinds of accommodations you need. One student needed faculty members to provide her with copies of notes because her learning disability made note taking very difficult. However, the faculty member worked with only the sketchiest of notes, making the accommodation difficult to meet. The adviser suggested that the faculty member get students in the class to agree to make copies of notes for this student, a request that they agreed to quickly. Another adviser got each student in a class to agree to read one article apiece for a visually impaired student because the reading service on campus was too far behind.

Advisers can help you understand how emotional stress may be contributing to your problems and get you connected to the student counseling center. They may know of economic resources available on campus if you are collapsing under your expenses. Some have been able to intervene with the business office around late bills until loan or scholarship monies come in.

Advisers also can help some students decide that the program isn't what they thought or that this isn't a good time for them to be pursuing the degree. A good adviser can help you decide if you made a mistake about the degree or the program and withdraw or whether what you need is a leave of absence. These are very separate decisions and should be made carefully rather than as a reaction to enormous feelings of frustration and rage. If you have a good adviser, it is worth sitting down and discussing why you applied, what your expectations were coming into the program, and what your current experiences are. Your adviser may help you understand whether your initial goals are truly incompatible with the goals you've established or whether it is a temporary problem related to specific courses.

What advisers will not or should not do is make excuses for you or attempt to make it possible for you to get through the program without getting an education. We have all had students who have claimed that the assignments were too difficult or that they were unable to understand core areas of the curriculum and expected their advisers to get them out of the work. This is clearly an unreasonable demand to make, and the best advise your adviser can give you is to withdraw before you invest any more time or money in a program you are not likely to succeed in anyway. It is advice you should listen to as well. We hope the adviser will also take the time to work with you around finding a better graduate field that matches your interest and abilities.

COMPETITION AMONG THE RANKS

Graduate education is competitive. In programs where men outnumber women, it is not uncommon for women to be encouraged to compete with each other rather than their male counterparts. This is generally a mistake. If the field is also dominated by men, then competing against other women ensures that women will remain at the lower levels in the profession. It is the nature of win-lose situations.

Options in Competitions, or Women Versus Women

Whenever possible, women should bolster their mutual performances by working together rather than trying to outdo each other. To accomplish this, you and your fellow women students should share knowledge among each other as comprehensively as possible about every aspect of the program. Second-year and above students should seek out first-year students to advise them about how women can best succeed in the program, by identifying women on faculty who will provide mentoring relationships, and by letting fellow women know what faculty members are most likely to cause women problems. The politics of success are usually based on the formation of coalitions, and women who unify to achieve rather than compete against each other have the potential of becoming a powerful presence in the program.

▨ Healthy and Unhealthy Competition

Many women, just like their male counterparts, are competitive, and it would be foolish for us to advise you to never compete against another woman in the program. Many women in graduate school are driven to be first in their class (this is the voice of experience), and they want to be the one that skews the grading curves. We are not suggesting that you should submerge your intellect or your competitive edge. It is what got you into graduate school in the first place, and it is what will keep you at the top of your field (if that's where you want to be).

We are suggesting that competition for the sake of beating others is neither healthy nor productive. For one thing, most graduates rely on fellow graduates at some point as referral sources or references. The more good will you generate with fellow students, the more helpful they will be, long after the last blue book in your life has been closed. Striving to be the best is desirable. Being the best by trashing your fellow students or by doing things that can sabotage the success of others provides short-term gains and long-term hostilities.

The question is how to remain competitive enough to keep a high standing in the program at the same time as you form coalitions. Earlier, we described how study groups are best when there is some complementarity among the members. The more balanced the needs are, the more the group as a whole can succeed. If you are good in math, another member has skills in presentations, and a third member is a first-rate editor, all of you are likely to have stellar academic careers because of your ability to enhance each other's skills. It is unlikely that all of you will perform at the same level, even with this arrangement, but all of you will perform better than without each other's help.

WHAT REALLY COUNTS

In the long run, what really counts is that all of you complete the program successfully. Academic relationships are a lot like work relationships. They have a kind of satisfying, but superficial, intimacy that lasts as long as you have school in common. They can then shift into a professional relationship or into memory.

If you are going to remain in the same community as most of your fellow students, then the level of competition should be enough to keep you where you want to be in your class but not at levels that others see as hostile. Remember the caveat about professions being like small towns: Bad behavior can haunt you long after your last A.

INDEX

ABOUT THE AUTHORS

Barbara Rittner is Associate Professor of Social Work at the University of Georgia. Previously, she was associated with Barry University in Miami, where she did her graduate work, and on faculty at the University of Nevada at Reno and the State University of New York at Buffalo. She is currently a member of the graduate faculty at the University of Georgia and serves on the Admissions Committee in the School of Social Work. She primarily teaches advanced graduate students. She has published numerous articles and book chapters on the issues of multiculturalism in education and on child welfare policy.

Patricia Trudeau is a counselor and instructor at Conestoga College in Kitchner, Ontario, Canada, and an instructor at the School of Social Work at the State University of New York at Buffalo. She has earned master's degrees in social work and adult education and counseling from the University of Toronto. Her professional career of nearly 20 years has enabled her to practice in a variety of settings, from social action to individual counseling and teaching. The primary focus of her current position is helping students have successful college experiences through improved interpersonal and academic skills.